THE HISTORY OF
Wars

THE HISTORY OF
Wars

KEN HILLS

CHERRYTREE BOOKS

Contents

A Cherrytree Book

Designed and produced by
A S Publishing

First published 1994
by Cherrytree Press Ltd
a subsidiary of
The Chivers Company Ltd
Windsor Bridge Road
Bath, Avon BA2 3AX

British Library Cataloguing in Publication Data

Hills, Ken
  Cherrytree History of Wars
  I. Title
  909

ISBN 0-7451-5180-9

Typesetting by Dorchester Typesetting Group Ltd, Dorset
Printed in Italy by Imago Publishing

Why Wars Happen

War is as old as human history. In the past 2,500 years the world has enjoyed peace in only one year out of twelve. Accounts of wars fill the historical books of the Old Testament. Classical literature abounds in tales of the battlefield. In China, between 722 and 464 BC, there were only 32 years of peace. Throughout the 16th and 17th centuries in Europe, there were only nine years without war. In the 1990s, the world is troubled by over 25 substantial conflicts.

Wars of conquest

Wars rarely have simple causes, but most wars, both in the past and now, have been wars of conquest, fought for territory, wealth and power. The ancient empires of Sumer, Assyria, Persia and Egypt; of India and China; Alexander's empire and the empires of Greece and Rome were won by conquest and maintained by war. In our own times, World War II was a war of conquest begun by Nazi Germany in an attempt to dominate the world.

Religious wars

There have been wars of conquest fought for religious reasons. The religion of Islam, founded by the prophet Mohammed, sprang to life in the 7th century AD in the sparsely populated Arabian peninsula. It became the driving force that created an empire. Within a century, Islamic armies had conquered lands that stretched from Spain to Central Asia and converted the subject peoples to Islam. Today, one-seventh of the world's population are Muslims.

Civil wars

Quarrels over political and religious beliefs between rival parties in the same country have inspired civil war. The English Civil War of the 17th century divided the country between those who supported the king in religion and politics and those who were prepared to risk life and freedom to oppose him. Spain's Civil War of the 1930s was fought between left-wing socialists and right-wing conservatives over who should govern the country and how it should be governed.

Wars of independence

The desire for freedom and self-government has led to wars of independence. In 1775, British colonists in North America went to war with their mother country for the right to govern themselves. In the 19th century, the peoples of Spain's South American empire won their independence by war.

Nationalism has been a frequent cause of wars of independence, particularly when great empires have been in decline. A war of independence, 1821-1832, won the Greeks their freedom from the Turkish empire. Modern Italy was born in 1861, after years of war against the declining empire of Austria.

Today, in the ruins of the former nation of Yugoslavia, rival groups slaughter each other without mercy, to win territory to establish themselves as new nations.

From the 11th century to this day, wars have been fought between Muslims and Christians. This knight was a member of the Knights Templar, an order of knights, half religious, half military, whose aim was to keep the Holy Lands of Palestine Christian.

The American Revolution was the first major war of independence in modern times. Settlers in colonial America objected to being taxed by the far-distant British government without being represented in parliament.

Whatever the causes of war, those who suffer most are the ordinary people who lose their homes, their happiness, their loved ones and sometimes their lives. After the prolonged war in Vietnam, thousands took to boats to try to find a safe refuge.

The Dawn of Warfare

The Wars of Egypt

Opposing sides Egyptians v Hyksos people of Kadesh in Palestine, then part of the Egyptian empire.
Causes The Hyksos rebel against their Egyptian masters. Thutmosis invades Hyksos territory, at the head of a large Egyptian army, to crush the rebellion.
Major figure Pharaoh Thutmosis III of Egypt.
Battleground Central Palestine.
Main events 1469 BC Thutmosis, with an army of 10,000, makes a rapid march into Palestine. Rebels gather at Megiddo, near Mount Carmel. Thutmosis, leading attack personally in his chariot, breaks through Hyksos outer defences and advances towards main Hyksos army drawn up near the fortress of Megiddo. Egyptians outflank Hyksos rebels and win complete victory. Megiddo, the first recorded battle in history, 1470-1450 BC. Thutmosis goes on to conquer new territory in Asia Minor and Mesopotamia. Egyptian fleet commands the Eastern Mediterranean.
Outcome Egypt the dominant power in Middle East for the next 100 years.

Assyria's Wars

Opposing sides Assyrians v Egyptians, Babylonians, Jews and Philistines.
Causes Assyrian ambition to build and maintain a large empire.
Major figures Kings of Assyria: Tiglath-Pileser III, Sargon, Sennacherib, Ashurbanipal.
Battlegrounds Middle East and Asia Minor.
Main events 745-727 BC Tiglath-Pileser overcomes all opposition in Mesopotamia and conquers Syria and Palestine. Maintains order in his empire by a policy of ferocious cruelty. 722 Sargon II extends Assyrian rule into central Anatolia (modern Turkey). 705 Sennacherib puts down rebellions in Palestine, Syria and Babylonia. 701 Fails to capture Jewish capital Jerusalem when army is stricken by plague. 689 Captures and destroys Babylon. 668-625 Ashurbanipal puts down repeated revolts in Egypt and Babylonia. 616 Assyria exhausted by years of conflict. Medes and Babylonians invade. 612 Assyrian capital Nineveh destroyed.
Outcome End of Assyrian power. Medes and Persians become dominant peoples in Middle East.

Thutmosis III, a brilliant general and pharaoh, led his troops into battle in his own one-man chariot.

The Assyrians drove three-man chariots. With a driver and shieldsman, the warrior (here the sovereign Ashurbanipal), was free to fire arrows, throw javelins and even fight with the two-headed axe.

The Greek and Persian Wars

1. The Marathon Campaign

Opposing sides Greek city states v Persia.

Causes Cities of northern Greece are part of Persian empire. They rebel and Athens supports their revolt. Persian emperor Darius determines to crush revolt and punish the Athenians.

Leaders Greece: Callimachus, Miltiades. Persia: Darius.

Battleground Greece.

Main events 499 BC City of Miletus, supported by Athens, leads revolt against Persia. 498 Rebels defeated in Battle of Ephesus. 494 Darius captures Miletus and revolt collapses. 490 Persian army crosses Aegean Sea to attack Athens. Half land at Marathon, about 42 km (26 miles) from Athens, to draw off Athenian army. Rest sail off to attack Athens from the sea. Athenian army, fewer than 20,000 men, led by Callimachus and Miltiades, attack Persians at Marathon and win complete victory. Pheidippides runs to Athens with the news (first Marathon run).

Outcome Temporary victory for Athens.

2. Campaigns of Thermopylae and Salamis

Opposing sides Athens, Sparta and cities of southern Greece v Persia.

Causes Revenge; Darius determined to get even with Athens for Marathon defeat.

Leaders Greece: Leonidas. Persia: Emperors Darius and Xerxes.

Battleground Greece. Strait between island of Salamis and Greek mainland.

Main events 490 BC Darius plans to conquer Greece, but revolt in Egypt 486-484 delays him. 486 Darius dies; succeeded by Xerxes. 481 Xerxes musters army of 200,000 men. 480 Persian army invades Greece; army carried by huge fleet of supply ships sailing along the shore. August: At Thermopylae, Leonidas, king of Sparta, with 6,000 men defends the narrow pass. Persians, helped by Greek traitor, find secret way through mountains and take Leonidas's men by surprise. Greeks wiped out and Leonidas killed. After their victory Persians occupy Athens. September: At Battle of Salamis, Greek warships sink half Persian supply fleet. Persian army, short of supplies, destroys Athens, then retreats.

Outcome Greece is saved.

The Wars of Alexander the Great

Opposing sides Greek states v Persia.

Causes Alexander's ambition to conquer Persia, the traditional enemy of Greece.

Leaders Alexander III (the Great) king of Macedonia. Darius III, Persian emperor.

Battlegrounds Asia Minor, Egypt, Palestine, Syria, Persia, India.

Main events 336 BC 20-year-old Alexander becomes king of Macedonia. In 334 leads combined Greek armies to conquer Persian empire. 333 Battle of Issus (in Syria). Alexander's army of 30,000 smashes Persian host of 100,000, losing only 450 men. Darius flees. 331 Alexander occupies Egypt. Meanwhile, Darius gathers huge army in Mesopotamia. Alexander hastens to confront him. 1 October: Battle of Gaugamela (near Nineveh); Alexander wins great victory. Darius murdered by own men. 331-330 Alexander pursues fleeing Persians. Destroys ancient Persian capital Persepolis. 328-327 Invades India. 326 Wins Battle of the Hydaspes (now Jhelum) River. Greeks refuse to go on and Alexander reluctantly retreats. 323 Alexander dies of fever in Babylon, aged 32.

Outcome Greek civilization spread by Alexander's conquests. But quarrels between his generals break up empire.

Led by the gallant Spartan king, Leonidas, a small Greek force held out for days against the Persians who attacked them as they tried to defend a narrow mountain pass at Thermopylae.

Alexander seemed to have no fear. Many tales are told of his exploits. He tamed a wild horse called Bucephalus that no one else dared touch. He rode the horse on his campaigns and, when it died, built a city in its memory.

The Roman Conquests

How Rome began

Rome began as a small village by the River Tiber in Italy. The Romans themselves dated their history from 753 BC, when, by tradition, Rome was founded by Romulus, a grandson of the Etruscan king of Latium. Etruscan kings ruled Rome and Latium until, in 509 BC, the Romans rebelled. They drove out King Tarquin and Rome became a republic.

Rome conquers Italy

At first, the new republic had to fight for its life against its neighbours. In 496 BC, at Lake Regillus, the Romans defeated a combined army of other Latin tribes. Their beaten foes were given fair treatment and became Rome's allies. During the next two hundred years Rome conquered Italy. Continuous war made the Roman army the finest in the world.

Foreign wars

Rome's wars of conquest continued beyond Italy and won her many enemies. King Pyrrhus, of Epirus in Greece, set out to crush the upstart Romans once and for all. In 280 BC he landed in Italy with an army and a squadron of war-elephants. Pyrrhus twice defeated the Romans, but lost so many men that he was forced to withdraw and return to Epirus.

Rome's next opponent was the North African trading city of Carthage. The seafaring Carthaginians dominated the western Mediterranean. The first Punic, or Carthaginian, War (264-241 BC) was fought between them and the Romans for control of Sicily.

The Romans realized that to defeat the Carthaginians they would have to beat them at sea. They had no navy, but starting from scratch the Romans built a

Map: The new republic of Rome was surrounded by enemies, many of whom had formed a league that hoped to conquer Rome. But the Romans fought them at Lake Regillus and later made alliances with them.

Rome's strength was her army. A Roman legionary often had to carry 30 kilograms of baggage on long marches. As well as sword, shield and javelin, a man might carry a pickaxe, a turf-cutter, a jar and bowl, a bedding roll and a bag of personal possessions.

ing up an empire in Spain. When they attacked the city of Saguntum, which was allied to Rome, the Romans declared war. So, in 218 BC, the second Punic War began. While the Romans were still preparing for war, a 40,000-strong Carthaginian army equipped with war-elephants set out overland to invade Italy. The army's leader, Hannibal, was perhaps the ablest general the Romans ever faced.

To Rome's consternation, Hannibal managed to get his

large war fleet which was soon able to match the Carthaginians in battle. However, Carthage was not easily overcome. A Roman army was defeated in North Africa and the Roman fleet sailing to its rescue was wrecked by a storm. The war for Sicily went on for another 13 years before the Carthaginians were finally defeated. Sicily then became Rome's first province.

Rome's greatest enemy
After losing Sicily, the defeated Carthaginians turned to build-

Hannibal was one of the best generals in history. Starting from Spain, with 40,000 men on foot or horseback – and 37 elephants – he crossed the Pyrenees, France and the Alps to reach Italy, where he inflicted several defeats on the mighty Romans.

The Romans had an effective way of shielding themselves from attacks from above. They used their shields to form a testudo (tortoise). This formation was so strong that, it was said, a chariot could be driven over the top.

Julius Caesar was a great general, statesman and historian. He conquered Gaul and invaded Britain. Immensely popular with the people of Rome, he was killed by enemies who feared that he wanted to be king.

army across the high mountain barrier of the Alps and into Italy. Within two months he had defeated two Roman armies sent to dispose of him.

The way to Rome was now open, but Hannibal lacked siege machines and dared not attack the city itself. Hastily, the Romans collected together another army, the largest in their history, to crush Hannibal and end the Carthaginian threat. It failed. In 216 BC, at Cannae, the Roman army suffered a bloody defeat.

Rome victorious

Elsewhere, Rome was victorious. A young 25-year-old general, Scipio Africanus, drove the Carthaginians out of Spain and landed in North Africa to attack Carthage itself. There he was faced by Hannibal, who had left Italy and returned to Africa to defend his native city. The two great commanders met in battle at Zama in 202 BC. Hannibal's army was cut to pieces and Carthage was at Rome's mercy.

Fifty years later, Carthage was strong enough to rebel again. The city held out against the Romans for three years, but in 146 BC it was finally and utterly defeated. The victorious Romans levelled Carthage to the ground. Meanwhile, the Romans had been fighting a different war, in the east, against Philip, king of Macedonia. In 197 BC a Roman army sent to Greece overwhelmed the Macedonians at Cynocephalae.

A second campaign followed and, at the Battle of Pydna in 168 BC, the power of Macedonia was finally destroyed.

With Carthage and Macedonia both overthrown, Rome virtually ruled the Mediterranean. Proudly, the Romans called it 'Our Sea'.

The republic in crisis

While the Romans were winning great possessions abroad, the government of Rome remained much the same. A host of problems arose. The institutions that had worked when Rome was a small city state could not cope with the task of running a huge empire. Politicians bickered while victorious army generals jockeyed for power.

Caesar's rise and fall

The greatest of these generals, Julius Caesar, was a member of an ancient Roman family. He had made his name with victories in Egypt and in 59 BC was elected to the Triumvirate, the group of three officials who ruled Rome.

From 58 to 50 BC Caesar won new lands for Rome. He conquered Gaul (France), Switzerland, parts of Germany and the Netherlands. In 55 BC and again in 54 BC he landed in Britain, but withdrew rather than risk a tiresome guerrilla war with the natives.

Octavius (Octavian), who ruled after Julius Caesar, was the first Roman emperor. He took the name Augustus, and the power that nominally belonged to the Senate and people of Rome, but he ruled wisely and brought peace to the expanding empire.

Map: At its greatest size, in AD 117, the Roman empire stretched from northern Britain to the shores of the Red Sea, and what is now the Gulf.

By 50 BC one member of the Triumvirate was dead. Pompey, the second, sided with the Roman Senate when it tried to strip Caesar of his military command. Civil war followed. Pompey was killed and Caesar became sole ruler of Rome. His rule lasted for only a year. In 44 BC he was assassinated by his enemies on the floor of the Senate.

The first emperor

Civil war followed Caesar's death. It ended in victory for Caesar's old party led by the renowned soldier Mark Antony and Caesar's adopted son Octavius. Their alliance was short-lived. They went to war to decide who should wield supreme power in Rome. The struggle ended in victory for Octavius at the sea battle of Actium in 31 BC.

The Romans were by now

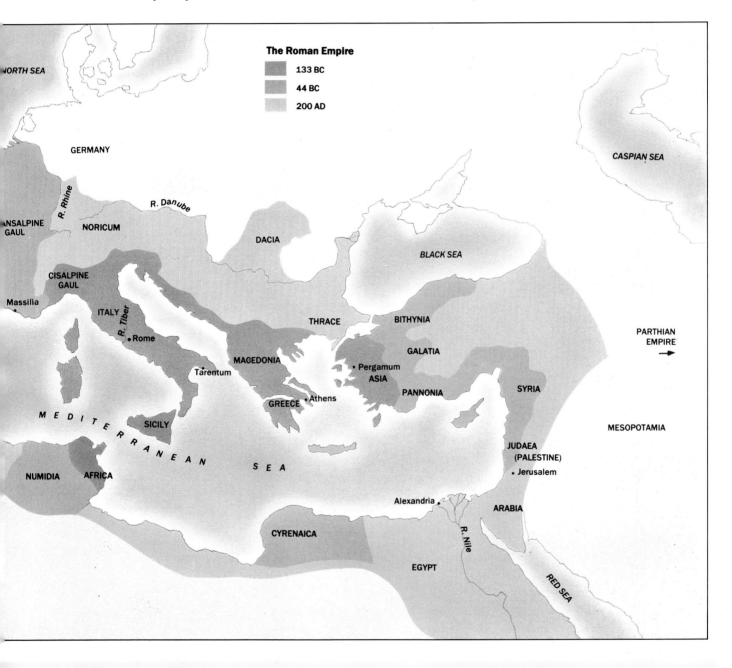

The Roman Empire

- 133 BC
- 44 BC
- 200 AD

NORTH SEA

GERMANY

R. Rhine

R. Danube

CASPIAN SEA

TRANSALPINE GAUL

NORICUM

DACIA

BLACK SEA

CISALPINE GAUL

Massilia

ITALY

R. Tiber

Rome

THRACE

BITHYNIA

PARTHIAN EMPIRE →

GALATIA

MACEDONIA

Pergamum

ASIA

SYRIA

Tarentum

PANNONIA

GREECE

Athens

MEDITERRANEAN SEA

SICILY

MESOPOTAMIA

NUMIDIA

AFRICA

JUDAEA (PALESTINE)

Jerusalem

Alexandria

ARABIA

CYRENAICA

R. Nile

RED SEA

EGYPT

heartily sick of war and were ready to accept any leader who promised them peace and good order. Octavius played on this war-weariness. Patiently and by degrees he introduced a new system of government which made him complete master of the Roman state. In 27 BC, aged 36, he took the title Caesar Augustus, emperor of Rome.

The peak of empire

For two hundred years after Octavius the empire enjoyed almost unbroken peace and prosperity. It continued to grow. Britain was added in AD 43. At its greatest extent in AD 117 when Emperor Trajan died, the empire stretched from the Atlantic coast of Britain to the shores of the Red Sea in southern Arabia.

The empire at bay

Emperor Hadrian followed Trajan. He realized that the empire had become too large for its own good and cut it back to frontiers that the Roman army was able to defend. These frontiers lasted another hundred

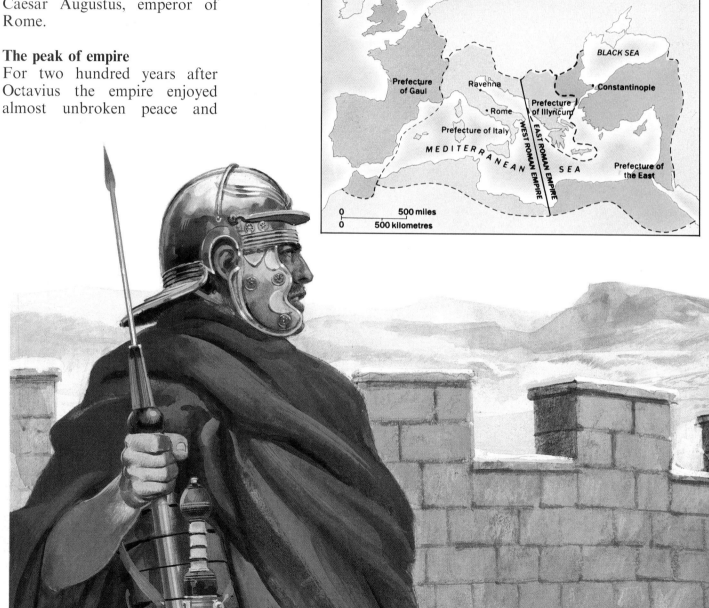

To prevent the warlike Picts invading the peaceful Roman province of Britannia, the emperor Hadrian built a wall across Britain. It was 80 Roman miles (120km) long, with a fort every mile. In about 150 years there were only two serious breaches.

Map: In AD 395 the Roman empire was split in two, each with an emperor. The Eastern empire was based on the city of Byzantium, which was renamed Constantinople after the emperor Constantine. Each of the new empires had two prefectures.

years. They were put to the test when barbarian German tribes from the north and the Sassanids from Persia in the east attacked the empire. Rebellions also broke out inside the empire, which the army, no longer the invincible force it once had been, was unable to put down. After the murder of Emperor Alexander Severus in AD 235, government broke down completely.

For a time, the empire was in danger of breaking up as leaders of the army in the provinces fought each other for power. It was saved by two outstandingly able emperors, Diocletian (284-305) and Constantine (306-337).

Diocletian reorganized every aspect of the administration and parcelled the empire out between four rulers. Constantine divided the empire in two, headed by two emperors. He himself took the eastern part, and between 224 and 330 made a magnificent capital for it at Byzantium, on the Black Sea. The rebuilt city (now Istanbul) was called Constantinople.

The end of the empire

The western empire, based on Rome, was eventually overrun by tribes of Angles, Saxons, Vandals and Goths. Some of these barbarian peoples settled as farmers while others came to plunder. Thousands more were employed by the Romans as soldiers to defend the empire against further attacks. In 410 and again in 455, Rome itself was occupied and looted. By 476 there was no longer a Roman empire in the west. It had gone, broken up into a patchwork of small barbarian kingdoms.

The eastern empire survived and for a time it flourished. As the empire of Byzantium, it lingered on for a thousand years after the empire the Romans created had vanished.

The Wars of the Dark Ages

The invasion of Britain

Opposing sides Romano-British v East
German tribes (Angles, Saxons and
Jutes).
Causes German tribes seeking land
and plunder in the rich island of
Britain.
Leaders German invaders: Hengist, Horsa,
Aesc, Cerdic, Ceawlin. Romano-British:
Vortigern, Ambrosius.
Battlegrounds Southern and eastern
England.
Main events Around 450 Jutish leaders
Hengist and Horsa overcome resistance
of British chief Vortigern and settle in
Kent. 457-473 Hengist and his son Aesc
drive out Britons and strengthen their
kingdom in Kent. 477 Saxon chief Aelle
lands in Sussex and drives Britons into
the forest of the Weald. 491 Aelle
captures stronghold of Pevensey and
kills all Britons there. 495-560 Cerdic
and his descendants establish kingdoms
in Isle of Wight and Wessex. Around 495
Battle of Mons Badonicus (Badbury, nr
Swindon). Britons under Ambrosius win
great victory. 560 Ceawlin becomes king
of Wessex. 577 Battle of Deorham
(Dyrham, nr Bath). Ceawlin defeats
British and reaches Bristol Channel.
Britons of Devon and Wales now cut off
from each other.
Outcome England becomes English.

Attila invades Europe

Opposing sides Huns (collection of tribes
from Central Asia) v Western Roman
empire.
Causes Attila's greed for plunder, loot and
land.
Leaders Attila, king of the Huns v
Theodoric, king of the Visigoths and
Roman general Aetius.
Battlegrounds France, Italy.
Main events 451 From his base in
Hungary Attila sets out to conquer
western Europe. He crosses the Rhine
leading a mounted army of 100,000 Hun
warriors. They advance across northern
France on a front 150 km (93 miles) wide
destroying everything in their path.
Aetius raises an army to fight them. 451
May: Attila besieges Orléans. Theodoric
joins Aetius with an army. Together they
approach Orléans. Attila retreats and
draws up his army at Châlons. 451 June:
Battle of Châlons. Theodoric killed in a
confused struggle but Attila beaten and
retreats across the Rhine. 452 Attila
invades Italy. Hun army crosses the Alps.
Lays waste northern Italy but is
weakened by famine and disease. Pope
Leo I bribes or persuades Attila to
withdraw. 453 Attila dies. His empire
falls apart.
Outcome Huns vanquished. Western
Europe saved from barbarian conquest.

The Wars of the Franks

Opposing sides Franks v Muslims.
Causes Muslim aim to conquer
France.
Leaders Franks: Charles Martel (the
Hammer), Charlemagne (Charles the
Great), Eudo, count of Aquitaine.
Muslims; Abd er-Rahman, governor of
Muslim Spain.
Battlegrounds France and Spain.
Main events 712 First raid into France by
Muslims from Spain. 721 Battle of
Toulouse, Franks under Eudo defeat
Muslims and drive them back to Spain.
725-726 Muslims return and occupy
lands in southern France. Their raids up
the Rhône valley reach Besançon. 732
Battle of Tours, major victory for
Franks. Charles Martel defeats Muslims,
Abd er-Rahman killed, Muslims flee in
panic. 771 Charlemagne becomes sole
ruler of France. 773-774 Charlemagne
conquers Lombardy and adds it to his
empire. 777-801 Franks under
Charlemagne conquer northern Spain.
800 Pope crowns Charlemagne Holy
Roman Emperor. 800-814 Charlemagne
defends his empire against a new threat –
Viking raids by sea and land.
Outcome Defeat of Muslim attempt to
conquer western Europe. Foundation of
the Holy Roman Empire.

The Siege of Constantinople

Opposing sides Byzantines v Arabs.
Causes Arab ambition to conquer
Europe and spread the Muslim religion.
Byzantines' fortress city of
Constantinople (modern Istanbul) guards
the invasion route into Europe.
Leaders Byzantium: General Leo. Arabs:
Generals Maslama and Suleiman.
Battleground Constantinople.
Main events 717 June: Maslama ships
80,000-strong Arab army across the

*The merciless Huns struck terror
wherever they went. They fought
ruthlessly, with no mercy for the weaker
tribes they overran. Attila attacked
both the Eastern and Western Roman
empires.*

Hellespont and attacks Constantinople. Leo beats off the Arabs, who suffer huge losses. September: Suleiman arrives with large reinforcements of men and ships. Leo attacks and drives off Arab fleet. 718 Spring: Arabs return to the assault aided by 50,000 reinforcements. Leo repels all attacks. Summer: Leo goes on the offensive; wipes out Arab fleet blockading Constantinople and defeats part of the Arab army. Bulgarian army comes to the aid of Byzantines and defeats Arab army at Adrianople. Arabs retreat. Storm destroys most of Arabs' remaining fleet.

Outcome Arab defeat saves Christian Europe from invasion by Muslim Arabs.

The Viking invasion of Britain

Opposing sides Vikings, sea raiders from Denmark, Norway and Sweden (also called Danes or Norsemen) v English.

Causes Vikings sought plunder and wanted to settle in England, a richer and more fertile land than their own.

Leaders Vikings: Guthrum. English: Alfred the Great, king of Wessex.

Battleground Wessex.

Main events 800-870 Frequent Viking raids along the coasts of England. 866 Danes capture York (Jorvik). 871 Wessex army under Ethelred and younger brother Alfred defeats invading Viking army at Ashdown. Alfred succeeds as king of Wessex. 878 Vikings under new leader Guthrum defeat Alfred at Chippenham. He escapes and hides on the island of Athelney in a maze of marshes in western Wessex. 878 With new army, Alfred defeats Guthrum at Edington. Treaty of Wedmore; Guthrum gives up conquest of Wessex. Vikings retreat and settle in eastern and northern England (the Danelaw). Alfred begins to build navy as protection against future Viking attacks.

Outcome Wessex, secure against further Viking attacks, became the base from which Alfred's successors conquered all England.

In 732 a Frankish army, led by Charles Martel, defeated a Muslim army at Tours, and prevented western Europe from being conquered.

The Vikings travelled in longships. They carried swords, spears and round shields, and wore helmets with metal nose protectors. The ships had carved prows and sterns, often shaped to look like the head and tail of a sea monster.

The Crusades

How the crusades began

Palestine and Jerusalem its chief city are sacred to people of three different faiths; Jews, Christians and Muslims. Many times during the past thousand years, members of those faiths have fought over this Holy Land.

In the 7th century AD, Palestine was settled by Arabic-speaking peoples. The Arabs were devout but tolerant Muslims. For centuries, they allowed Christian pilgrims to worship at the holy places of Palestine in peace.

Late in the 11th century, Palestine was conquered by the Seljuk Turks. They were also Muslims but were less tolerant. They ill-treated Christian pilgrims and soon the pilgrimages stopped altogether.

Tales of Turkish cruelties outraged the Christians of Europe. Over the next 200 years they attempted to drive the Muslims from Palestine by means of military expeditions called crusades.

The People's Crusade

In 1095, Pope Urban II called on Christians to drive out the Turks. His appeal whipped up religious frenzy in Europe. Noblemen raised armies while wandering preachers carried the pope's message to the people. A priest named Peter the Hermit gained a large following. In April 1096, he and his unruly supporters set out across Europe looting as they went. At Constantinople the Byzantine navy ferried them to the other side of the Bosphorus, where they made camp in a deserted fortress. A Turkish army was waiting for them. Foolishly, many of Peter's men rushed out to meet it and were overwhelmed. Only a few escaped and returned to Europe to tell the tale of their disaster.

The First Crusade

Armies formed by the nobles of France and Germany reached

Christian pilgrims catch a first glimpse of Jerusalem, the Holy City sacred to Jews, Christians and Muslims. The crusades began when Palestine was conquered by Seljuk Turks, who were less tolerant than the Arab Muslims, who had left the pilgrims in peace.

passed before the Christians were able to break out and march on.

In June 1099, the crusaders laid siege to Jerusalem. The Muslims held out for nearly a month, but on 14 July the city walls were breached. The crusaders swarmed in and, as at Antioch, massacred the helpless inhabitants.

The land of Outremer

After the fall of Jerusalem most of the crusaders returned to their own countries. Those who remained settled in 'Outremer', the name they gave to Palestine. They divided it into four states: Edessa, Tripoli, Antioch and Jerusalem.

The Christian settlers had seized the land from its Muslim inhabitants and were always in danger of being overwhelmed by them. To meet this threat, they formed societies of men who lived like monks but fought like soldiers. The most powerful of these groups were

Constantinople in April 1097. They crossed the Bosphorus, captured Nicaea and defeated a Turkish army at Dorylaeum.

The next part of the route to the Holy Land ran through the city of Antioch. The crusaders captured it with ease, for Christians living there secretly opened one of the gates. The crusaders poured in and slaughtered the Muslim inhabitants. Another Muslim army arrived and besieged the city with the crusaders inside it. A year

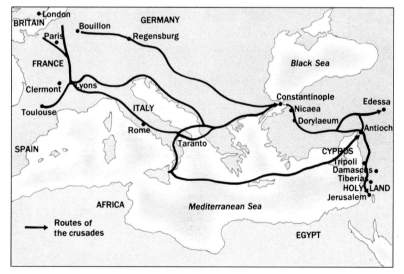

The crusaders arrived at Jerusalem in June 1099 and made their major attack on 14 July. It took less than two days for the bloodthirsty Christians to break down the city walls and begin their slaughter of the inhabitants.

Map: The early crusaders went overland to Palestine because the ships of the time were too small and primitive to carry thousands of men and their supplies. Later they took ship from Venice.

the Hospitallers and the Templars. The Muslims hated and feared them more than any other Christians.

The Second Crusade

In 1144, the Turks reconquered Edessa. The Christians of Outremer were threatened and appealed to the Christians of Europe to come to their aid. Pope Eugenius III took up their cause. Aided by Bernard of Clairvaux, the leading churchman of the age, he persuaded the kings of France and Germany to join in a Second Crusade to defend the Holy Places of Outremer.

The two armies marched away in the late summer of 1147. For both, it was a disastrous journey. The Germans were defeated at Dorylaeum by the Turks while the French were severely mauled passing through enemy territory on the way to the Holy Land.

The battered remnants met in Syria in summer 1148. With incredible folly, their leaders decided to attack the city of Damascus, whose king had hitherto been friendly to them.

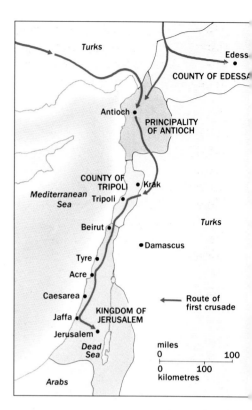

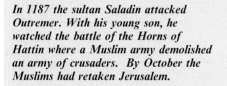

In 1187 the sultan Saladin attacked Outremer. With his young son, he watched the battle of the Horns of Hattin where a Muslim army demolished an army of crusaders. By October the Muslims had retaken Jerusalem.

Map: Some of the victors of the First Crusade settled in the land they had conquered, which they called Outremer. This consisted of four states: Edessa, Antioch, Tripoli and Jerusalem. All around these states, the Muslims waited for their revenge.

After five days of half-hearted assaults they gave up the siege. The demoralized crusaders straggled back to Europe.

The Third Crusade

In 1187, under a new leader, Saladin, Sultan of Egypt and Syria, the Muslims captured Jerusalem and destroyed a Christian army at the Battle of Hattin. To Christians in Europe the loss of Jerusalem was a calamity and the pope called for a Third Crusade. A combined force of French and English gathered in Sicily. In spring 1191, they took ship for the Holy Land.

The crusaders began by capturing the port of Acre. The French king Philip Augustus then returned to France leaving Richard I of England as the crusaders' leader. At Arsuf his army swept aside Muslims who were barring the way to Jerusalem. But Richard knew his forces were too weak to take the city. In September 1192 he made peace with Saladin and left the Holy Land for ever.

The Fourth Crusade

In 1198, Pope Innocent III appealed for another crusade to the Holy Land. But those who answered his call were more interested in plunder than in recovering Jerusalem.

The Venetians alone possessed a fleet able to carry the Christian army across the Mediterranean, but their price for doing so was more than the crusaders could afford. The two parties therefore struck a deal.

They agreed to seize Constantinople, capital of the Byzantine empire, the wealthiest city in the world. The loot from its capture would meet the cost of hiring the fleet and leave plenty over for all concerned.

The Knights of St John took their name from the hospital of St John in Jerusalem where pilgrims and crusaders could rest and recover. Their name, emblem and charitable work live on to this day in the St John Ambulance Brigade.

In July 1203, the fleet landed near Constantinople and the Christians began their attack. For some months the defenders beat off all assaults, but in the following April the attackers broke through the walls. They ravaged the great city, slaughtered its people and carried off most of its riches. Laden with plunder, the crusaders gave up all idea of freeing Jerusalem and returned to their homelands.

The Children's Crusade

Children, too, caught the religious frenzy of the age. In the summer of 1212, child preachers persuaded thousands of other children to join in a crusade. The French children went to Marseilles, where a pair of rascally merchants offered them free passage to Palestine. Some were drowned on the voyage; the rest were sold as slaves. The German children got no farther than Italy. Penniless and

starving they had to beg to stay alive. Very few ever came home again.

The later crusades

In 1217, Christians from many nations gathered at Acre for a fifth crusade. They planned first to occupy Egypt and make it their base for an invasion of Outremer. The crusaders took a year to capture Damietta, a town guarding the way into Egypt. Pushing on up the River Nile, they blundered into a trap set by the Egyptians. That was the end of the crusade. The

The Fourth Crusade planned to finance an attack on Egypt by looting the fabulously wealthy city of Constantinople. Aided by the Venetians, the crusaders ran through the city, seizing everything of value and slaughtering the inhabitants.

These French children, marching with the crimson banner of St Denis, left their homes in the summer of 1212 to 'recapture the Holy Land for Christ'. Nearly all of them perished, along with thousands of other children from elsewhere in Europe.

peacefully what years of war had failed to achieve.

Jerusalem was retaken by the Muslims in 1244. Four years later, led by Louis IX of France, the Seventh Crusade set out to regain it. Egypt was the first objective. The crusaders succeeded in advancing up the Nile, but as they went, the Egyptians blocked the river behind them. Cut off from supplies, the crusaders had to surrender. Louis and his army were taken prisoner. The crusade ended in total failure.

crusaders were forced to accept humiliating surrender terms and had to retire.

The army of the Sixth Crusade, led by Frederick II of Germany, arrived in Outremer in 1228. Both Christians and Muslims were weary of war by this time and chose to talk rather than fight. Frederick was one of the ablest men of the age. By skilful negotiation he regained Jerusalem for the Christians and won a 10-year treaty of peace. The crusade was a triumph for Frederick. His clever bargaining had won

The end of the crusades

In 1260, Baybars became sultan of Egypt. One by one the crusader fortresses of Outremer fell to him. When he died in 1277, only Tripoli and Acre remained in Christian hands.

After a 12-year truce, war began again in 1289. Tripoli soon fell to the Muslims and Acre, the last Christian foothold in Outremer, was lost in May 1291. Its fall ended the crusaders' dream of a Holy Land ruled by Christians where pilgrims could travel in peace.

The city of Acre was the last Christian stronghold left in Outremer. In 1291 the Egyptian sultan Baybars sacked the city. The remaining crusaders were slaughtered or sold as slaves, and Outremer ceased to exist.

23

The Hundred Years War

How the war began

The Hundred Years War was not a single conflict. It was a series of wars between England and France which began in 1337 and ended in 1453.

The wars were fought to decide who should rule France. Edward III, king of England in the early 14th century, was lord of Gascony and Guyenne in southwestern France. He was bent on enlarging his French dominions, but more than that, he claimed to be the rightful king of France itself. Philippe VI of France naturally opposed Edward's claim to his throne and strove to drive the English out of France altogether.

The Battle of Sluys

In 1337, a French army invaded Edward's French possessions. Edward retaliated by proclaiming himself king of France. From bases in Flanders he launched a series of raids into Philippe's territory.

On 24 June 1340, an English fleet crossing the Channel carrying Edward and his army clashed with a French fleet off the port of Sluys. In minutes, hundreds of the French had been struck down by English arrows. As ships of the two sides came together, English men-at-arms poured on to the French ships and finished off the survivors. Sluys gave England command of the sea.

Henceforth, Edward could land his troops on the French coast where and when he pleased.

The Crécy Campaign

The English raids into northern France continued and led to the first major land battle of the war. In summer 1346, an English army under Edward and his son the Black Prince was trapped by the French near the village of Crécy. The English were greatly outnumbered but had no choice but to stand and fight. The battle was fought on 26 August. Fifteen times the heavily armoured French knights charged the English, only to be mown down in the arrow-storm fired by the Black Prince's Welsh archers. Crécy was a total English victory.

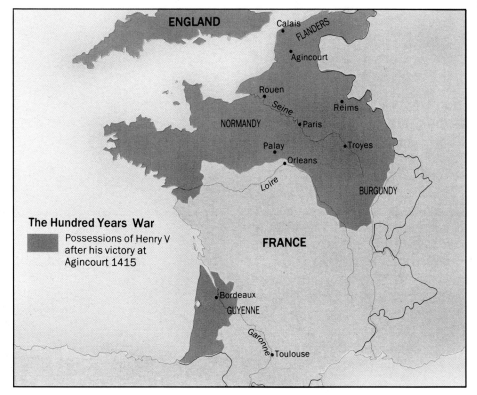

The Hundred Years War
Possessions of Henry V after his victory at Agincourt 1415

The Black Prince was the eldest son of the English king Edward III. An inspiring leader in his time, he achieved little beyond victories in battle. He died before his father, so his son became king as Richard II.

Map: At the beginning of the Hundred Years War, English possessions in France were small. But Edward III, who was married to the sister of three French kings, claimed the throne of all of France, and fought to increase his territory there.

In August 1347, the English took Calais. The port became an English town and served as England's gateway to France for more than 200 years.

Wars are expensive. Edward could no longer afford to keep an army in the field and in September 1347 he signed a truce with France.

Poitiers

In 1347, both England and France were victims of the Black Death, a dreadful plague that killed a third of the people of both countries. War was resumed in 1355, and in the following year the Black Prince led a raid into central France from the English territory of Guyenne. A large French army arrived on the scene and the prince ordered a retreat. But weighed down with loot, the English were overtaken near the town of Poitiers.

The Battle of Poitiers was fought on 19 September. The English were victorious and the French king John II was captured. However, once again Edward ran out of funds to keep the war going and peace was signed at Bretigny in 1360. The treaty recognized King Edward's rights to his French lands while Edward himself gave up his claim to the throne of France. King John was released in return for three million gold crowns.

Calais was beseiged by Edward III for a year. The inhabitants were starved into surrender. To save their fellows, six barefoot burghers (townsmen) are reputed to have presented themselves and the keys of the city to Edward. They wore nooses round their necks to show their readiness for death. The intervention of Queen Phillipa saved their lives.

young and ambitious Henry V became king of England. At the time France was weakened by civil war. Henry seized the opportunity to renew the English claim to the French throne.

In 1415, Henry invaded northern France and captured Harfleur. Marching towards Calais the English were intercepted at Agincourt by a French army that greatly outnumbered them. At Agincourt, on 25 October, the French army was cut to pieces once again by the English archers. The French lost more men than Henry had in his entire army. Normandy was occupied by the English and, in 1420, the Treaty of Troyes ended the war.

The treaty forced Charles VI of France to recognize Henry as

The French recovery

After Poitiers the power of France revived while that of England declined. Bertrand du Guesclin, one of the finest soldiers of the age, transformed French military tactics. He captured English strongholds one after another, until only Calais and a few other coastal towns remained in English hands. In 1372, England lost the naval Battle of La Rochelle and, with it, command of the sea. Both the Black Prince and his father the king fell sick. The Prince died in 1376 and his father a year later.

Henry V and Agincourt

A lull in the fighting lasted nearly 40 years, but in 1413 the

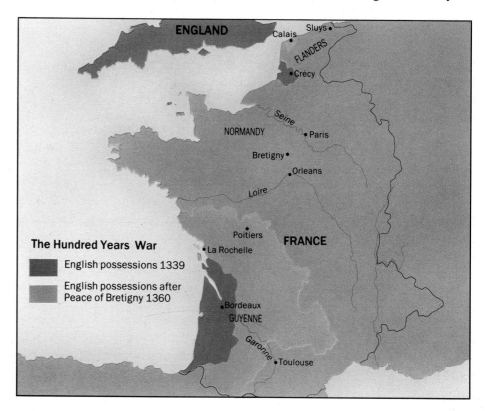

The Hundred Years War

■ English possessions 1339

■ English possessions after Peace of Bretigny 1360

At Agincourt an English force of 13,000 men, spurred on by Henry V, won a decisive victory over 50,000 French. The battlefield was muddy from rain and the French cavalry, wearing heavy armour, became bogged down, and unable to flee from a hail of English arrows.

Map: Henry V greatly expanded English territory in France and also became, until his death, the agreed heir to the French throne. But, thanks to Joan of Arc, the crown returned to a French monarch, and by 1453 only Calais remained in English hands.

his heir. And Henry married Katherine, Charles's daughter. But Henry did not live to claim the throne of France. He died on 31 August 1422.

Joan of Arc

The civil war in France continued after Henry's death and the English were able to add to their territory. By 1428, they were laying siege to the city of Orléans.

In 1429, a 17-year-old French peasant girl named Joan of Arc presented herself to the true heir, Charles's son, the dauphin. She convinced him that God had inspired her to drive the English from France and that he, the dauphin, would be crowned its rightful king.

The dauphin put Joan in command of an army. At its head, she raised the siege of Orléans and, a month later, defeated the English at the Battle of Patay. Joan's successes showed that the English could be beaten. French morale soared and, on 16 July 1429, the dauphin was crowned King Charles VII of France.

Joan's career was nearly over. In 1430 she was captured by a party of England's Burgundian allies. They turned her over to the English, who accused her of witchcraft. She was tried and found guilty. In May 1431, Joan was burned to death as a witch in the market place of Rouen.

The French triumph

The English did not prosper after Joan's death. Their alliance with Burgundy ended and they faced France alone. The French regained Normandy. Then they invaded Guyenne and, in July 1453, French heavy guns won the Battle of Castillon.

On 19 October 1453, the English lost Bordeaux, their last major stronghold in western France. Its fall ended the Hundred Years War. Only Calais remained in English hands.

Joan of Arc raised the siege of Orléans. Appearing with her great white banner, she put heart into the French troops. In the thick of the fighting, without shield or sword to protect her, she urged on the soldiers even after she was wounded.

The Wars of the Middle Ages

The Norman Conquest

Opposing sides Normans v English.
Causes Rival claims to the English throne. After King Edward the Confessor dies, Harold earl of Wessex makes himself king of England. William duke of Normandy (the Conqueror) also claims the throne.
Leaders Normans: Duke William. English: King Harold II.
Battleground Southeastern England.
Main events 1066 Summer: William gathers an army in Normandy. He waits for the winds to turn and blow his invasion fleet across Channel. Early September: King Harald Hardrada of Norway with Harold's brother Tostig invades northern England. Harold hurries north. He wins the Battle of Stamford Bridge: Harald Hardrada and Tostig killed. 28 September: Wind has changed. William's army crosses Channel. Harold's army races 400 km (248 miles) south to meet them. 14 October: Battle of Hastings; Harold killed. William wins complete victory. After the battle, William advances on London; is crowned king of England in Westminster Abbey on Christmas Day.
Outcome English suffer harsh Norman rule. England united under a line of strong kings and gains links with rest of Europe.

Genghis Khan and the invasions of China

Opposing sides Mongolia v Chin and Hsia empires of China.
Causes Genghis Khan's aim to conquer China.
Leaders Genghis Khan, Mongol emperor. His son Ogotai.
Battlegrounds Western and northern China.
Main events 1211 Genghis invades China. 1213 Mongol armies reach the Great

Wall. 1215 Mongol hordes lay waste northern China. They capture and plunder Beijing. Chin emperor recognizes Genghis Khan as his overlord. 1224 Chin and Hsia make an alliance and rebel against Mongols. 1225 Genghis picks his son Ogotai to succeed him and lead Mongol armies. 1226 Ogotai gathers army of 180,000 men and moves south into China. Battle of the Yellow River: Mongols defeat Chin/Hsia army, 300,000 strong. 1227 Mongols pursue enemy; destroy Hsia capital, Ningshia, and capture Hsia emperor. Genghis sets out to return to Mongolia but dies on the way.
Outcome Death and destruction in the conquered territories. But once resistance crushed, the Mongols maintained peace within their huge empire.

The Mongol invasion of Europe

Opposing sides Mongols v Eastern and central Europe.
Causes Mongol emperor Ogotai aims to conquer Europe.
Leaders Mongols: Ogotai, his son Kaidan and grandson Kaidu, General Subotai v King Boleslav of Poland. King Bela of Hungary.
Battlegrounds Russia, Hungary, Bohemia, Austria.
Main events 1237 Ogotai sends an army under Subotai from Mongolia to conquer central Europe. In two years, Mongols overrun most of Russia. 1240 They capture Kiev. Two Mongol armies advance across Europe. 1241 March: The northern force under Kaidu crushes King Boleslav's Polish army at Cracow. 9

Genghis Khan, which means universal or invincible lord, was the title taken by Temujin, the outstanding leader of the small Mongol tribe that he made into a nation and led to conquer China. Superb horsemen, the Mongols formed a highly disciplined and efficient army.

April: Battle of Leignitz. They trap the Silesian army and destroy it. 11 April: Southern Mongols led by Subotai and Kadan slaughter King Bela's Hungarian army in the Battle of Mohi. 1242 Combined Mongols threaten western Europe, but news arrives of death of Emperor Ogotai. By Mongol law, when a ruler dies his family must gather in Mongol capital Karakorum to elect his successor. Entire Mongol force makes the 10,000 km (6,000 mile) return march to Karakorum.
Outcome Western Europe saved by luck.

Kublai Khan and the invasion of Japan

Opposing sides Mongol empire in China v Japan.
Causes Intention of Mongol emperor Kublai Khan to add Japan to his empire.
Major figure Emperor Kublai Khan.
Battleground Islands of northern Japan.
Main events 1274 Kublai Khan collects an invasion fleet in Korea. It sails and captures small islands of Tsushima and Iki. Japanese defenders fight to the death. Mongols land on main island of Kyushu. While Japanese attack a storm threatens to destroy Mongol fleet. Mongol army retreats to ships and when storm has passed sails away. 1281 Kublai Khan prepares a much larger force to attack Japan. It sets sail for Kyushu. Fierce sea battles between Mongol fleet and Japanese defenders. Mongol army lands and meets desperate Japanese resistance. Violent storm wrecks the invasion fleet. Mongol army cut off. Japanese defeat and destroy it.
Outcome Japanese saved from Mongol conquest and remain independent and isolated from rest of world. They call the storm which delivered them 'kamikaze', the Divine Wind.

The Fall of Constantinople

Opposing sides Byzantium v Ottoman Turk empire.
Causes Ambition of Ottoman rulers to expand empire and force Christians to become Muslims.
Leaders Byzantine emperor Constantine XI v Ottoman emperor Mohammed II.
Battleground Constantinople (modern Istanbul).
Main events 1453 Mohammed leads army against Constantinople. 5 April: Ottomans besiege the city. Their great cannon knock holes in defences, but Byzantines beat off every attack. 29 May: From early morning Ottomans launch repeated onslaughts against weakest part of walls. Defenders exhausted by ceaseless attacks gradually give way. Constantine killed fighting on the walls. Ottomans plunder Constantinople for three days and slaughter Christian leaders. Mohammed converts the great Christian church of Hagia Sophia into a Muslim mosque.
Outcome End of Byzantine empire. Constantinople becomes capital of Ottoman Turk empire. Ottomans now poised to launch attacks into Europe.

The Wars of the Roses

Opposing sides Two noble English families and their allies: the house of York (white rose) and the house of Lancaster (red rose).
Causes Rivalry for the throne of England.
Leaders Lancastrians: Henry VI, Henry Tudor (later King Henry VII) v Yorkists: Edward (later Edward IV), Richard duke of Gloucester (later Richard III). Richard earl of Warwick, the 'Kingmaker', first Yorkist then Lancastrian.
Battleground England.
Main events 1455 First Battle of St Albans. Yorkists win, Henry VI captured. 1459 Warwick defeats Lancastrians at Blore Heath. 1461 February: Second Battle of St Albans. Lancastrians win, Edward of York escapes. He beats Lancastrians to London. He is proclaimed king as Edward IV. March: Yorkists win Battle of Towton. 1461-1471 Confused fighting over much of England. Warwick changes sides; he joins Lancastrians. 1471 April: Battle of Barnet; Yorkist Edward IV wins, Warwick killed. May: Yorkist victory at Tewkesbury confirms Edward on the throne. Henry VI murdered. 1483 Edward IV dies. His brother succeeds as Richard III. 1485 Lancastrian Henry Tudor returns from exile. Richard defeated and killed at Bosworth. Henry Tudor succeeds as Henry VII.
Outcome Strong monarchy and stable government re-established. Tudor dynasty rules until 1603.

Richard III goes into his final battle at Bosworth Field with his crown in place. His defeat brought to an end the Wars of the Roses and the reign of the Plantagenets. Richard was succeeded by Henry VII the first Tudor king.

The Thirty Years War

A war of religion and politics

The Thirty Years War was not one long unbroken conflict but a series of wars fought over a 30-year period. Most of the fighting was in Germany.

Religion was the original cause of the war. The Holy Roman Empire had been founded by Charlemagne in AD 800 as successor to the empire of ancient Rome. For centuries, its emperors had been appointed by election, but by the 17th century the title had become the permanent possession of the Austrian Habsburg dynasty.

Catholics versus Protestants

The core of the empire was Austria, Bohemia and the various states of Germany. Several of the German states and much of Bohemia had become Protestant during the Reformation, whereas Austria and the Habsburgs remained Catholic. The Thirty Years War began when the emperor tried to force Catholicism on his Protestant subjects.

The Protestants were supported by France, Sweden, Denmark and Holland. The Habsburgs were allied to the Catholic princes of Germany and to the Habsburg kings of Spain.

In its later stages, the war developed into a struggle for the leadership of Europe between

two royal dynasties – the Habsburgs of Austria and the Bourbons of France.

The war started in Prague in 1618. The following year Protestant nobles of Bohemia defied their new Catholic king, Ferdinand, and threw two of his officials and their secretary out of a high castle window. They followed this by deposing Ferdinand and putting Frederick, a German Protestant prince from the Rhineland, in his place. After early successes the rebels were routed at the Battle of the White Mountain in 1620, by an Imperial army under Count Tilly. Frederick fled and Ferdinand was restored to the Bohemian throne.

The Danish phase 1625-1629

In 1625, King Christian IV of Denmark invaded Germany as an ally of the German Protestants. On 24 August 1626, he lost the battle and half his army

at Lutter. More defeats followed. Finally, the imperial forces commanded by the mercenary general Count Wallenstein drove him back into Denmark. The Peace of Lübeck, signed on 7 June 1629, transferred substantial territories in Denmark and northern Germany to Catholic rule.

The Swedish phase 1630-1634

The inroads made by the Catholics in northern Germany greatly alarmed the Protestants of nearby Sweden. In July 1630, the Swedish king, Gustavus Adolphus, the ablest military commander of the time, landed with an army in Germany to restore Protestant fortunes. On 17 September 1631, he defeated a Catholic army under Tilly at Breitenfeld, near Leipzig. A year later, Gustavus was killed, on 16 November, at the Battle of Lützen.

Ferdinand II ruled the Holy Roman Empire from 1619. A fervent Catholic, he defeated many rebel nobles. In 1635 he succeeded in getting Catholics and Protestants to sign the Peace of Prague. But by the time of his death in 1637, fighting had broken out again.

Count Albrecht Wenzel Eusebius von Wallenstein commanded an army of volunteers and mercenaries who fought with General Tilly. Suspected of treachery, he was assassinated – probably on Ferdinand's orders – in 1634.

King Gustavus Adolphus of Sweden was nicknamed the 'Lion of the North'. He defeated General Tilly at Breitenfeld but lost his own life at Lützen. Here he shows off an invaluable innovation, light guns that could be moved swiftly round the battlefield.

The death of Gustavus was a disaster for the Protestant cause. On 6 September 1634, the imperial army, reinforced by 20,000 Spaniards, overwhelmed the Swedes at Nördlingen.

After nearly 20 years of almost constant warfare, both Protestants and Catholics were eager to end the fighting. On 30 May 1635, the Peace of Prague brought the second phase of the war to a close.

Habsburg against Bourbon: 1635-1648

The leadership of the Protestants now passed to France. France was a Catholic country.

King Louis XIII of France and Cardinal Richelieu his chief minister had no interest in the welfare of German Protestants. Their concern was to check the growing power of the Austrian and Spanish Habsburgs. From this point, the main issues in the war were political rather than religious.

In June 1635, five separate French armies invaded Spanish Habsburg dominions in the Netherlands, Germany and Italy. In 1636, northern France was invaded by an army from the Spanish Netherlands. The following year, a second Spanish invasion force crossed the Pyrenees into southern France. Meanwhile, a Swedish army had driven the imperial forces from the eastern German province of Brandenburg. By 1637, the Swedes were threatening Leipzig in the south. The warring

A French force lays waste to a German village. Town and country alike were ravaged by the continual warring. Innocent people lost their lives or livelihoods at the hands of ill-disciplined soldiers.

Cardinal Richelieu was the most powerful man in France and wanted France to be the most powerful nation in the world. Despite his position in the church, he happily allied France with Protestant Sweden and other states, in the interests of reducing Habsburg power.

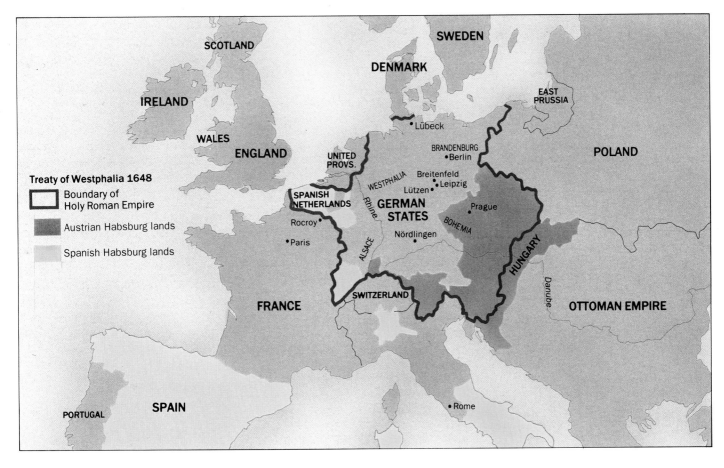

The outcome of the war

armies spread wholesale destruction across Germany.

The Spanish attacks on France became a war of sieges of border fortresses. Major battles were rare, but in May 1643 a French army led by the young Duc d'Enghien routed a Spanish invasion army, at Rocroy on France's eastern frontier.

Peace talks began in 1644. They proceeded very slowly and were not completed until, on 24 October 1648, the Treaty of Westphalia ended the war between France and the empire of Austria. The war between France and Spain continued until 1659.

The outcome of the war

The national boundaries settled by the treaty lasted virtually unchanged until the 19th century. France won most of what she had fought for in the war. She gained control of the important province of Alsace and the power of her Habsburg enemies had been greatly diminished.

The treaty recognized the Netherlands and Switzerland as independent sovereign states and confirmed the independence of the various states of Germany from the authority of the Habsburg emperors. Christian minorities were granted some measure of protection, thus marking the beginnings of religious tolerance.

The Holy Roman Empire continued, but in name only. Its authority and the reason for its existence had gone.

The war was a catastrophe for Germany. The damage it caused was unevenly distributed, but it is likely that the German population fell by nearly a half. Famine, plague and all manner of diseases were widespread. Whole towns and villages were plundered; some not once, but several times. Few wars in history have left behind them so strong a memory of horror and irreparable disaster.

Map: It took four years to negotiate the Peace of Westphalia. By its terms, Sweden and France extended their territory. Habsburg power was diminished. Switzerland and the Netherlands became independent. Nonconformist religions were recognized.

33

The Age of Kings

The Spanish conquest of America

Opposing sides Spanish adventurers v Aztecs of Mexico and Incas of Peru.
Causes Spanish greed for plunder and desire to convert American people to Christianity.
Leaders Spain: Hérnando Cortés, Francisco Pizarro v Aztec emperor Montezuma, Inca emperor Atahualpa.
Battlegrounds Mexico, Peru.
Main events 1. Mexico: 1518 Cortés and 600 men land in Mexico. They defeat Aztecs, capture Montezuma and occupy Aztec capital Tenochtitlán. 1520 Aztecs rebel. Spaniards driven from Tenochtitlán but murder Montezuma. 1521 Spaniards destroy Tenochtitlán and found new capital, Mexico City.
2. Peru: 1531 Cortés lands in Peru with fewer than 200 soldiers. 250,000-strong Inca armies oppose them. 1532 Incas terrified by Spanish guns and men on horses. Spaniards capture emperor Atahualpa by treachery. 1533 Spaniards murder Atahualpa. 1535-1536 Incas rebel but Spaniards overwhelm them. Spaniards now control entire Inca empire, and remain until 1826.
Outcome Spaniards destroy Aztec and Inca civilizations and enslave the people. Spain enriched by wealth plundered from American empire.

The Wars of Suleiman the Magnificent

Opposing sides Ottoman Turkey v Hungary, Austria, Knights of St John Hospitallers.
Causes Turkish aim to conquer central Europe.
Leaders Turkish sultan Suleiman the Magnificent v Austrian prince Ferdinand of Habsburg; de L'Isle Adam Grand Master of the Knights of St John.
Battlegrounds Hungary; Austria; Rhodes.
Main events 1522 June: Suleiman sets out to capture the island of Rhodes, stronghold of Knights of St John. September: Assault continues until December. Over 50,000 Turks killed. 20 December: Peace agreed. Surviving knights allowed to leave, Turks occupy Rhodes. 1526 Suleiman invades Hungary. August: he wins Battle of Mohács. 1529 Suleiman invades Hungary again. He captures Buda and advances towards Austrian capital, Vienna. September: Turks surround Vienna. Defenders fight off Turkish attacks. Winter approaches, Suleiman withdraws and Austrians pursue. 1532 Suleiman's second attempt to capture Vienna fails. Peace signed with Ferdinand of Habsburg.
Outcome Temporary halt in struggle between Austrians and Turks for domination of central Europe.

The Mogul conquest of India

Opposing sides Mogul kingdom of Kabul v peoples of northern India.
Causes Aim of Mogul king Babur and his descendants to win an empire in India.
Leaders Moguls: Babur, Humayan, Akbar v Ibrahim sultan of Delhi, Rana Sanga king of the Rajputs, Sher Shah emperor of Delhi.
Battleground Northern India.
Main events 1525 Babur invades northern India. 1526 He defeats Sultan Ibrahim at Panipat, occupies Delhi and founds Mogul empire. 1527 March 16: Battle of Fatehpur Sikri; Babur defeats Rana Sanga's Rajput army of 100,000 men. 1528-1529: Babur conquers Bihar and Bengal. 1530 Babur dies. His son Humayun becomes king. 1537-1539: Sher Khan leads revolt against Humayan. He drives Humayan out of India and becomes emperor as Sher Shah. 1545 Sher Shah dies. Turmoil in the empire. 1555 Humayan returns to reconquer empire. 1556 He dies. His son Akbar succeeds him. November: Second Battle of Panipat; Akbar wins and reoccupies Delhi. 1562-1567 He conquers Rajputana and wins support of local princes. 1600 Akbar extends Mogul empire over whole of northern India. 1605 Akbar dies.
Outcome Mogul empire lasts until overcome by the British.

The Aztecs thought that Cortés might be a god. Their emperor Montezuma welcomed him with gifts. In return Cortés imprisoned the emperor, stole his gold, and destroyed his temples.

The Spanish Armada

Opposing sides Spain v England.
Causes Two Spanish aims: to restore
 Catholic religion in England and end
 English attacks on Spanish shipping.
Leaders England: Queen Elizabeth I,
 Francis Drake v Spain: King Philip II,
 duke of Medina Sidonia.
Battlegrounds English Channel, North Sea.
Main events 1586 Philip begins building
 fleet to invade England (the Armada).
 1587 Drake raids Cadiz harbour. He
 destroys 33 Armada ships. Invasion
 delayed. 1588 July: Armada of 130 ships
 carrying 8,000 sailors and 19,000 soldiers
 sails to invade England. Armada loses six
 ships to English action. Sails up English
 Channel and anchors off Calais. At
 night, English send in fire ships and
 throw Spaniards into confusion. English
 pursue. Winds blow Armada northwards.
 Medina Sidonia decides to return to Spain
 by sailing right round British Isles.
 English use up all ammunition and give
 up chase. Armada ships battered by
 storms. Barely half return. September:
 Surviving ships stagger into Spanish ports.
Outcome England remains Protestant.
 Spain no longer regarded as unbeatable.

The English Civil War

Opposing sides King Charles I's
 supporters (Royalists) v Parliament,
 Merchants (Puritans).
Causes Quarrels over taxes and
 religion.
Major figures King Charles I, his nephew
 Prince Rupert v Generals Oliver
 Cromwell and Sir Thomas Fairfax.
Battlegrounds England and Scotland.
 Royalist Headquarters – Oxford;
 Parliament – London.
Main events 1642 Battle of Edgehill.
 Inconclusive, but Royalists continue
 advance on London. 1643 Scots enter
 war on Parliament's side. 1644 Battle of
 Marston Moor. Parliamentary/Scottish
 army under Cromwell defeats Royalists
 under Rupert. 1645 Parliament raises a
 new, highly trained army; the 'New
 Model Army'. Battle of Naseby. New
 Model Army crushes Royalists. 1645-
 1646 Royalist resistance collapses. 1646
 Charles taken prisoner. 1649 Charles
 tried and executed for treason.
Outcome Monarchy abolished. England
 becomes a republic, called the
 Commonwealth, but remains under
 military rule.

The War of the League of Augsburg

Opposing sides France v England, Spain,
 Holland, Austria, German states.
Causes Louis XIV attempts to dominate
 Europe. Neighbouring rulers alarmed
 and go to war to prevent him.
Leaders King Louis XIV of France;
 Marshal Luxembourg v William III, king
 of England and Stadtholder (ruler) of
 Holland.
Battlegrounds Mainly the Netherlands.
 Also battles at sea.
Main events 1688 French invade Germany.
 1689 Grand Alliance formed against
 France. 1689 August: Allies win Battle of
 Walcourt. 1690 Luxembourg defeats
 allies at Fleurus. July: French win naval
 Battle of Beachy Head. 1692 French seize
 fortress of Namur. May: Anglo-Dutch
 fleet defeats French at La Hogue. Louis
 gives up plan to invade England. 1693
 Luxembourg routs allied army under
 William of Orange at Neerwinden. 1695
 Luxembourg dies. 1695 William
 recaptures Namur. 1696 Stalemate in
 land warfare. Both sides seek peace.
Outcome 1697 Treaty of Ryswick; war
 decides little. Both sides agree to give up
 territory acquired in war but main
 problems remain.

*Elizabeth I inspired her navy to defeat
the Spanish Armada, offering to join
them in the fight: 'I know I have but the
body of a weak and feeble woman, but I
have the heart and stomach of a King,
and a King of England too.'*

*Roundheads (Parliamentarians) and
cavaliers (Royalists) fought it out
during the English Civil War. Oliver
Cromwell's 'New Model Army' was a
professional force, less colourful but
more effective than the Royalist
regiments.*

The American War of Independence

European colonies in America

In the mid-18th century Great Britain's colonies in North America stretched from French-owned Canada in the north to the Spanish colony of Florida in the south.

The French and Indian War

During the 1750s, French colonists began to move south into the valley of the Ohio River. The British regarded these settlers as a threat to their interests and sent troops under the command of Lieutenant-Colonel George Washington to bar further French advance. Native Americans played an important part in the war that followed, for both the British and French had formed alliances with local Indian peoples.

Two years later, when France and Britain joined opposite sides in the Seven Years War, the conflict in North America became an all-out struggle for control of the continent. Britain emerged victorious and, in 1763, at the Treaty of Paris which ended the war, they gained most of the French possessions in North America.

The road to rebellion

The British colonists could only deal with local affairs. All major matters, including taxation, were controlled by the British parliament in London. Britain was deeply in debt after

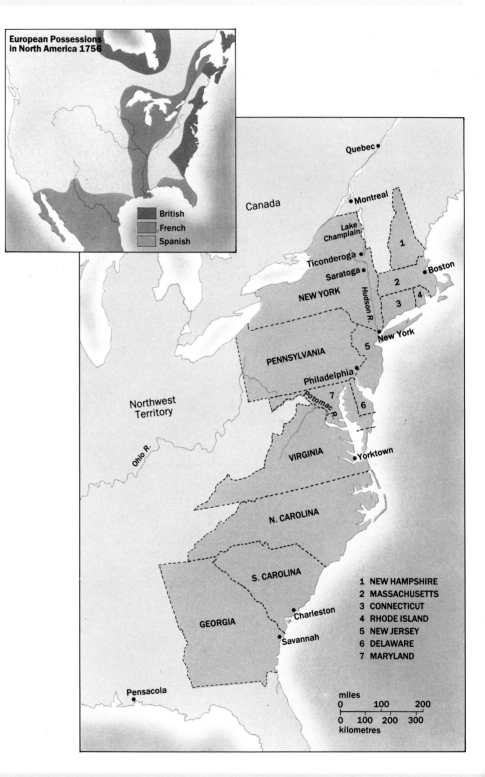

Top map: The territory governed by three colonial powers in North America in 1756 at the start of the Seven Years War. At odds with each other in Europe, Britain, France and Spain extended their disputes across the Atlantic.

Map: The thirteen colonies that eventually became the United States. In 1756 all were under British control though New York and New Jersey were originally settled by the Dutch, and Delaware by the Swedes. Canada remained in French hands until 1759.

the war. The British government therefore decided to tax the colonists in America in order to pay for the cost of the troops stationed there to protect them. Accordingly, in 1765, parliament in London passed the Stamp Act, which taxed

imposed on a variety of imports, including everyday needs such as tea.

The Boston Tea Party

The taxes led to widespread unrest. Matters came to a head in December 1773, when a

Thomas Gage was appointed governor of Massachusetts, which in effect placed the colony under military rule. In response, representatives from the colonies met in Congress in September 1774 and passed a resolution demanding that the detested Acts should be repealed. They also advised Americans to prepare for war.

The first shots

Hundreds of colonists became part-time soldiers. They were ready to fight at a minute's notice and were known as 'minutemen' for that reason. They soon showed how effective they could be.

In April 1775, the British garrison at Boston heard that the colonists were stockpiling arms at the towns of Lexington and Concord. British troops set out to seize these illegal hoards, but messengers from Boston raced ahead with the warning that the soldiers were on the way.

newspapers and various legal documents used in the colonies.

The Stamp Act angered the colonists so much that the British had to repeal it a year later. However, they persisted in their revenue-raising policy. In 1767, new duties were

party of colonists disguised as Mohawk Indians threw a cargo of tea into Boston Harbour. This act of defiance exasperated the British. To teach the Americans a lesson they rushed several more repressive measures through parliament. General

To the Americans, tea was an emblem of British oppression. The Boston Tea Party was a gesture of defiance. Patriots disguised as Indians boarded British ships in Boston Harbour and dumped a cargo of tea.

An infantryman of Washington's 'American Continental Army'. In the early days of the war, the Americans had no uniforms. They were encouraged to wear brown by Congress, but most of the colonies had their own colours. The British wore red.

command. The British garrison in Boston attacked the colonists dug in on high ground overlooking the city and drove them off, but at the fearful cost of over a thousand casualties.

The Siege of Boston

In July 1775, General Washington took command of the American volunteer fighters around Boston. He spent the first six months training and organizing them into something resembling an army. Early in 1776, Washington succeeded in placing his artillery on the Dorchester Heights to the south of Boston where it could bombard the British fleet. General Howe, the British commander, realized he had been outmanoeuvred. His entire force, plus those colonists who had remained loyal to Britain, abandoned Boston and left for Canada aboard a fleet of British transports.

There was a brief skirmish at Lexington and both sides suffered their first casualties. At Concord the British found that the arms stored there had vanished. Their return march was a nightmare. They were sniped at by the minutemen for most of the way and nearly 300 men were killed or wounded. It was the beginning of the War of Independence.

Congress chooses Washington

The Congress met again in May 1775. Members from the different colonies voted to combine their forces in a single 'American Continental Army'. It was to be commanded by a wealthy Virginian plantation owner, Colonel George Washington.

The Battle of Bunker Hill

The war's first battle was fought in June 1775, before Washington had taken up his

The fighting spreads

Congress now decided to attempt to drive the British

George Washington was 43 when he took command of the army. He was a prosperous landowner, able to forgo pay and charge his expenses only. Tall and impressive to look at, he was a fine horseman and had fought bravely during the French and Indian Wars.

The Congress appointed a committee to draft the Declaration of Independence. Its members were (left to right) Thomas Jefferson, Benjamin Franklin, Roger Sherman, John Adams and Robert Livingston. The Declaration was published on 4 July 1776.

from Canada. An American army crossed the border and, in December 1775, attacked the city of Quebec. The assault failed. British reinforcements arrived the following spring and forced the Americans to withdraw. Canada remained British.

The Declaration of Independence

By mid-1776, most Americans were in favour of complete separation from Britain. In June, a committee appointed by Congress drafted a document that affirmed both the independence of America and the principles the new country stood for. The final version of this 'Declaration of Independence' was published on 4 July. The day is now celebrated as a public holiday in the United States.

The New York campaign

Meanwhile, a 30,000-strong force of British troops and German mercenaries had landed at New York. The British, led by Howe, began by capturing Long Island.

Washington conducted a skilful withdrawal, but was forced to abandon New York. Harried all the way by the enemy, he retreated with the remains of his army across the River Delaware to Pennsylvania. It was the lowest point in Washington's career.

The tide begins to turn

Howe withdrew to winter quarters in New York leaving a detachment of Germans at Trenton to keep watch on the Americans. Washington decided to surprise them. On Christmas night 1776, his army crossed the Delaware and fell upon the unsuspecting foe. The attack was a success and a thousand Germans were captured.

Two British columns set out to box the Americans in, but Washington gave them the slip. On 3 January 1777, at Princeton, his men routed one part of the divided enemy force before retiring to Morristown for the winter.

Assuming that fighting would be suspended until spring, Howe's main forces were in winter quarters. Washington chose Christmas night 1776 to recross the Delaware River and surprise the Germans, who had been left to watch the Americans.

The Northern Campaign and Saratoga

In spring 1777, the British planned an attack from Canada. An invasion force led by General Burgoyne captured Fort Ticonderoga on 7 July. Burgoyne moved farther down the Hudson River, hoping to link up with Howe, but unknown to him Howe was off hunting Washington. By this later to enter the war on the American side.

In autumn 1777, Howe's army landed from the sea and captured Philadelphia, the American capital. He and his troops sheltered there during the winter. A few miles away, Washington's army, cold and hungry, shivered in the snow at Valley Forge. Many of the troops died.

made war on British shipping. Their raids had had little effect on the progress of the war. The British could still blockade the American coast and land troops where they wished. So long as they were able to do this, they were unbeatable.

In 1778, France entered the war on the American side. From that point onwards Britain's command of the seas

time, the British had come too far to return. They were isolated and outnumbered and at Saratoga, on 17 October, Burgoyne was forced to surrender.

The American victory at Saratoga was a turning point in the war. It persuaded the French to give formal recognition to the United States and

Two years of confused warfare followed. The centre of the fighting shifted to the south, where, in May 1780, the Americans lost Charleston to the British.

The French and the war at sea

From 1776 onwards, American armed merchant vessels had

off America was challenged. When the British lost it, they lost the war.

Yorktown

In early 1781, the British general Cornwallis set out to occupy Virginia. He made Yorktown on Chesapeake Bay his chief base. Meanwhile, a

The winter of 1777 was a bleak time for Washington. Camped in the open at Valley Forge, a quarter of his troops died of cold and hunger. But he had a secret weapon in the shape of Baron von Steuben, who drilled the remaining troops into a formidable force.

French defeated a British fleet outside Chesapeake Bay. The British ships withdrew, leaving Cornwallis's army cut off by land and sea.

The British in Yorktown were now isolated and outnumbered. Cornwallis tried to break out but failed. On 19 October, he surrendered.

Peace

Peace talks began soon afterwards, but fighting went on for another year. A treaty signed in Paris finally ended the war on 3 September 1783. The United States was now an independent country. It extended from the Atlantic to the Mississippi and from Canada to Florida. In 1789, George Washington was chosen to be the new country's first president.

French army came down from the north and joined up with Washington's men. Together the combined force surrounded Yorktown. On 5 September, the

A sea battle off the coast of England. John Paul Jones, an American captain, refused to surrender to the English vessel HMS Serapis. Supported by a French ship, he managed to grapple and board the English vessel. As his own ship sank, he sailed to France with the English one.

The British surrender at Yorktown ended the war. General Cornwallis pleaded illness and sent a deputy to hand over his sword to Washington. But Washington refused to deal with a subordinate and watched as his deputy received it.

The French Revolution

The origins of revolution

By 1789, years of war and bad government had made France bankrupt. An unfair tax system demanded exorbitant taxes from the less well-off, while the rich nobility and clergy paid very little. Meanwhile, King Louis XVI and his court lived at Versailles in open and extravagant luxury.

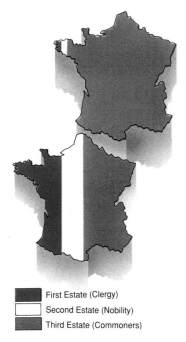

First Estate (Clergy)
Second Estate (Nobility)
Third Estate (Commoners)

That summer, the country became almost ungovernable as poor people rioted throughout France. In desperation, the king summoned the States General – a kind of national parliament representing all classes of the French people – to find ways of raising the extra money needed to solve the country's problems.

The beginnings of revolution

The States General met at Versailles in May. The representatives of the Third Estate, the common people, demanded a new constitution which would reform taxation and change the way France was governed. When the king refused, they defied him. They declared themselves the National Assembly and took an oath to remain together until their claims had been met. The king gave in and agreed to their demands.

The citizens of nearby Paris were celebrating this victory when news came of royal troops marching against them. At once, Paris began to prepare for battle. On 14 July, a mob stormed the royal fortress of the Bastille for the ammunition kept there and captured it.

On 4 August, the National Assembly abolished the ancient

Maps: Disproportional representation! The First and Second Estates numbered only half a million out of a total 25 million people (top), yet each estate had the same number of seats in the States General.

The Bastille was a royal fortress, where for centuries French kings had imprisoned people without trial. It was a symbol of oppression and injustice. On 14 July 1789, the citizens successfully stormed it.

privileges of the nobility and clergy. Soon afterwards, rumours went round that nobles close to the king were scheming to overthrow the Assembly. At this, an angry crowd, mostly of women, marched out to Versailles. They seized the king and his family and brought them back to Paris.

The king's escape plan fails
After two years of semi-captivity the royal family made an attempt to escape and find refuge abroad with the queen's brother, the emperor of Austria. On 20 June 1791, in disguise, the royal party managed to give their captors the slip and head for the frontier. Bystanders at the nearby town of Varennes saw through their disguise and they were hustled back to Paris in disgrace.

The revolutionary wars begin
The new Assembly which met in October was dominated by a party of extremists called the Jacobins. Led by Maximilien Robespierre, the Jacobins swiftly eliminated the moderates who opposed them. Many opponents fled abroad. In April 1792, the Assembly declared war on Austria for aiding French exiles who were plotting against France.

The end of the monarchy
An Austrian army invaded France and was soon marching on Paris. Its commander threatened to destroy Paris if the royal family was harmed. Hearing this, the Parisians concluded that the king was in league with

Louis XVI might have made good his escape if he had not travelled in a bright yellow coach drawn by six horses, and if the queen had not taken trunkfuls of clothes, two maids and a hairdresser.

Maximilien Robespierre caused thousands of his fellow countrymen to be guillotined during the Reign of Terror. He met the same fate himself in 1794.

the enemy. On 10 August 1792, the royal family narrowly escaped death at the hands of a furious mob as they fled to seek safety with the Assembly.

The Convention, a new form of Assembly, was elected. Many of its members were enemies of the king and in September they abolished the monarchy. But ex-king Louis had not long to live. Letters were found proving that he had plotted against the Revolution. He was tried for treason, and on 21 January 1793 he was executed at the guillotine. In October, the queen met the same fate.

Crowds of people came to the executions at the guillotine. The women of Paris were always there. Many of them sat where they could get the best view and did their knitting as they watched. Their name tricoteuses *means knitters.*

Many innocent citizens were condemned to the guillotine by Revolutionary Committees, which staged trials of those who were suspected of plotting with enemies abroad to overthrow the Revolution.

The Reign of Terror

In the late spring of 1793, the Revolution was near to being overthrown. France was in extreme danger. An Austrian army was camped on French soil. Food was short.

Hostility to the Revolution was widespread and in places there was open revolt. In April, the Committee of Public Safety was formed to root out opponents of the Revolution and raise armies to defend France. Headed by Robespierre, the Committee ruled by fear. People were arrested on any suspicion. Over two thousand in Paris alone died at the guillotine during the year of the Terror.

By summer 1794, the French had defeated the invaders. Robespierre then suffered the same fate that he had inflicted on others. His former friends turned against him. He was tried and found guilty of crimes against France. He and other leaders of the Terror were guillotined on 28 July. The Reign of Terror was over.

The reaction

The French people were by now weary of the Revolution. A reaction against much of what it had stood for set in. The Convention was abolished and France was run by a group of five 'Directors'. Their rule was corrupt and inefficient and they came to rely on the army to keep them in power.

Enter Napoleon Bonaparte

The armies the revolutionaries had created became the best in Europe. Their most successful commander was Napoleon Bonaparte. In 1799, when the Directory was dissolved, he became one of the three Consuls appointed to rule France. He returned to the battlefield and defeated Austria and her allies in a series of military campaigns which made France the most powerful country in western Europe. Napoleon now had no rival. On 18 May 1804, he crowned himself emperor of France.

The Wars of the 18th Century

The Great Northern War

Opposing sides Russia, Poland and Denmark v Sweden.

Causes Russia and allies set out to crush Sweden and end Swedish dominance of the Baltic.

Major figures Peter the Great, tsar of Russia v King Charles XII of Sweden.

Battlegrounds Denmark, Norway, Baltic States, Finland, Poland, Russia.

Main events 1700 Charles invades Denmark. Danes beaten and get out of war. 1700 Battle of Narva (Estonia). Charles defeats huge Russian army. 1701 Battle of Riga; Charles defeats Russian/Polish army and invades Poland. 1702-1706 Swedes subdue Poland. 1703 Peter founds St Petersburg and gives Russia an outlet to Baltic Sea. 1708 Charles invades Russia. Russians retreat, destroying everything as they go. 1708/1709 Swedes perish in Russian winter. 1709 Battle of Poltava. Swedes routed; Charles flees. Russia occupies Poland. 1714-1718 Charles raises new army, invades Danish Norway, shot dead at Fredriksten. 1721 Swedes exhausted. Ask for peace.

Outcome Russia replaces Sweden as dominant power in the Baltic; becomes major European power.

The War of the Austrian Succession

Opposing sides Austria, Britain, Hanover, Holland v Bavaria, Prussia, France, Spain.

Causes 1. Other powers dispute Maria Theresa's right to inherit Habsburg Empire. 2. Britain and France fight for control of India and North America.

Leaders Maria Theresa v Frederick the Great of Prussia.

Battlegrounds Europe and America.

Main events 1740 Maria Theresa inherits Habsburg Empire. 1740 Frederick invades Austrian Silesia. 1742 War spreads to Bohemia and Bavaria. 1743 Anglo-Dutch army beats French at Dettingen. 1745 Austrians overrun Bavaria. French invade Flanders. They fight indecisive Battle of Fontenoy with British. In America, British capture Louisbourg from French. Frederick defeats Austrians in Bohemia. 25 December: Treaty of Dresden. Frederick gains Silesia and quits war. In India, French capture Madras from British. In Europe, French invade Holland. 1747 British win naval battle off Cape Finisterre against the French. 1748 Treaty of Aix-la-Chapelle ends war.

Outcome Austria weakened by long struggle. Prussia becomes major European power.

The 'Forty-five' Rebellion

Opposing sides English and Scots loyal to the Hanoverian kings (Loyalists) v English and Scots who wished to restore the Stuart dynasty to the throne of the United Kingdom.

Causes Stuart attempt to regain the throne. Leaders: King George II, the duke of Cumberland v Charles Stuart, the 'Young Pretender' (Bonnie Prince Charlie).

Battlegrounds Scotland, northern England.

Main events 1745 July: Charles lands in western Scotland. He has no army, but Scots Highlanders flock to support him. They capture Scots capital Edinburgh and win Battle of Prestonpans. November: Charles invades England. His army reaches Derby and causes panic in London. George II prepares to leave. But the English do not join Charles as he had hoped. A loyalist army approaches. Charles retreats to Scotland. He wins Battle of Falkirk. 1746 16 April: Loyalist

Peter the Great at Poltava, scene of a great victory. To make Russia a world power, Peter needed to reduce Sweden's power and gain access to the sea. He was successful in both his aims, winning the Baltic ports of Riga, Reval and Viborg and the war with Sweden.

drive them out of Germany. Frederick's magnificent army now crippled by years of fighting. 1760 Russians and Austrians make sudden attack. They seize Berlin and burn it. Frederick wins at Torgau, but his army further weakened. Both sides exhausted by fighting. 1762 New tsar Peter III takes Russia out of war. 1763 Peace comes at Treaty of Paris.
Outcome Both sides return territory seized during war.

2. The War in North America (French and Indian War)

Opposing sides Britain v France both with American Indian allies.
Causes British and French fight to drive each other out of North America.
Leaders British general Wolfe v French general Montcalm.
Battlegrounds Canada and northern New England.
Main events 1756 Montcalm attacks British positions south of Lake Ontario. 1757 He takes Fort William Henry. 1758 British capture Louisbourg but fail to take Fort Ticonderoga. 1759 British advance threatens French Canada. Wolfe captures Quebec. Both he and Montcalm killed. 1760 British capture Montreal.
Outcome French surrender Canada.

3. The War in India

Opposing sides Britain v France and Indian allies.
Causes British aim to drive France out of India.
Leaders British Robert Clive v Indian Surajah Dowla.
Battleground India.
Main events 1756 Dowlah captures Calcutta, chief town of British India. 120 British die in Black Hole of Calcutta. 1757 Clive defeats Dowlah's French/Indian army at Plassey. 1759 French fail to take Madras. 1760 British defeat French at Wandiwash and capture main French base at Pondicherry.
Outcome Britain becomes dominant power in India.

army led by Cumberland routs Charles's army at Battle of Culloden. Charles flees and escapes to France.
Outcome Hanoverians safe on UK throne. Stuart attempt to regain it finally fails.

The Seven Years War

1. The War in Europe

Opposing sides Prussia, Britain, Hanover v Austria, France, Russia, Sweden, Spain.
Causes Rivalry between Prussia and Austria.
Leaders Prussia's King Frederick the Great v Empress Maria Theresa of Austria.
Battlegrounds Europe east of River Rhine.
Main events 1756 Frederick invades Saxony. 1757 He invades Bohemia, defeats Austrians and besieges the capital, Prague. Combined French and Austrian army strikes back and threatens Frederick's capital Berlin. 1757 Frederick wins brilliant victories at Rossbach and Leuthen. 1758 He defeats Russian army at Zorndorf. 1759 A Prussian/British army beats French at Minden but fails to

Bonnie Prince Charlie, with his Jacobite followers, fully expected to seize the throne of Britain from the Hanoverians. But the duke of Cumberland exacted terrible revenge at Culloden, killing even the wounded on the field of battle.

In 1755, during the French and Indian Wars, Major General James Braddock, leading a British army, was ambushed by a combined force of French and Indians and forced to retreat.

The Napoleonic Wars

Nicknamed the 'little corporal', Napoleon was only 157 cm (5ft 2ins) tall. But what he lacked in stature, Napoleon made up for in courage and leadership. He was a general at 26 and at 35 became emperor of France.

In 1804, after the chaos of the French Revolution, Napoleon Bonaparte crowned himself emperor of France. A brilliant general, he fought and conquered most of Europe.

Napoleon's triumphs: 1805

The campaign of 1805 was the most brilliant of Emperor Napoleon's career. In October 1805, he defeated the Austrians under General Mack at Ulm. On 2 December, he crushed the main Austro-Russian army at Austerlitz. The Austrians surrendered on 4 December and the survivors of the beaten Russian army retreated to Russia. At the Treaty of Pressburg, France gained substantial territories in Germany and Italy from Austria.

The war at sea

Although they were masters on land, the French were beaten at sea. On 21 October 1805, a British fleet commanded by Admiral Horatio Nelson destroyed the combined navies of France and Spain in a battle off Cape Trafalgar. Nelson was killed, but his victory was decisive. It gave Britain command of the sea not only for the rest of the war but for the next hundred years.

Napoleon's triumphs: 1806-1807

Dismayed by Napoleon's irresistible progress, Prussia and

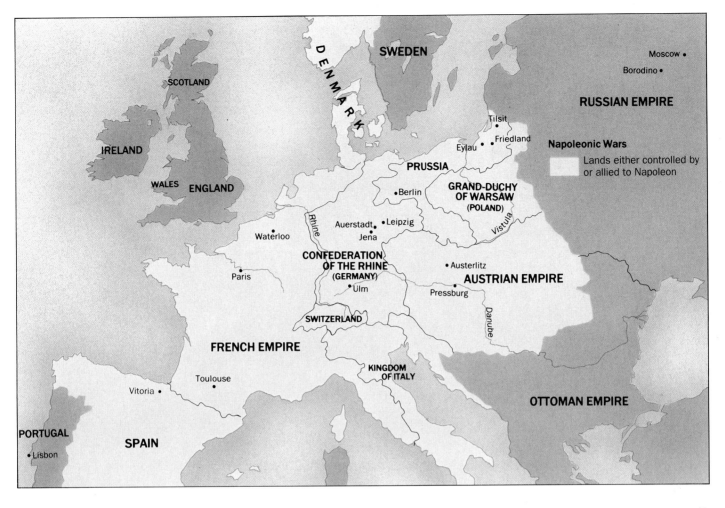

Saxony, in alliance with Britain, prepared for war against him. Napoleon lost no time in confronting these new enemies. On 14 October 1806, in separate battles at Jena and at Auerstadt, the French destroyed two Prussian-Saxon armies. On 24 October, they seized Berlin, the Prussian capital.

To thwart any Russian attempt to come to Prussia's aid, Napoleon advanced into Poland to the line of the River Vistula.

The Russian attack came in the depth of winter. The Battle of Eylau, fought on 8 February 1807, was inconclusive. Both sides went into winter quarters to prepare for the fighting to come.

War was resumed in late spring. The opposing armies met at Friedland on 14 June and again Napoleon won the day. The Russian army disintegrated and the Russian tsar Alexander asked for a truce.

The Treaty of Tilsit signed on 9 July ended the war. Prussia lost all territories in western Germany to France. Her lands in Poland were taken away to form an independent Grand Duchy and she was forced to pay France a fine of 140 million francs. Russia had to recognize the new Poland and became France's ally in the continuing war with Britain.

Tilsit was the crowning point of Napoleon's career. It made him ruler of most of Europe.

Economic warfare and the invasion of Russia

In 1806, Napoleon issued orders banning the import of British goods into all French-controlled territories. The British retaliated against this so-called 'continental system'. In 1807, they blockaded the

Map: Between 1799 and 1812, Napoleon conquered most of Europe. After his retreat from Moscow, he was defeated at Leipzig in 1813 and lost the French throne. Returning from exile in Elba, he raised another army in 1815 and was finally beaten at Waterloo in Belgium.

coast of Europe in order to stop all sea-borne trade with Napoleon's empire. The Russian economy was crippled by these restrictions and, in 1810, the Russian tsar Alexander reopened his ports to British goods. This action was a major breach of the continental system and Napoleon decided that Russia must be made to toe the line.

Invasion of Russia

In June 1812, leading an army 450,000 strong, he invaded Russia, driving the Russian army before him. On 14 September, after winning the Battle of Borodino, Napoleon entered Moscow.

Retreating from Moscow at the start of winter, Napoleon's army had no supplies. Soldiers and horses died in their thousands. Including those who were captured or deserted during the campaign, fewer than half of the original troops survived.

As they fell back the Russians had destroyed everything that might be of use to the invaders. The Grand Army found itself deep in enemy territory, short of supplies and without food or shelter. Winter was near and Napoleon decided he must retreat. In freezing weather and attacked all the way, the French died in their thousands. On 8 December, Napoleon himself left for Paris to raise another army. Barely a tenth of the Grand Army returned to France.

By April 1813, Napoleon had recruited another 200,000 men and marched them eastwards to join the remnants of the Grand Army.

War in the Spanish Peninsula

At the same time as these great events in eastern Europe and Russia were happening, the French were locked in a conflict with the British in Spain and Portugal. In 1807, with Spanish permission, a French army crossed Spain and occupied part of Portugal. The following June, Napoleon overthrew the monarchy in Spain itself and placed his brother Joseph on the Spanish throne.

The Spanish people rebelled and, in September 1808, the British landed to support them. Their stay was short-lived, for the French forced them to evacuate the following January.

In April 1809, Sir Arthur

Wellesley (later duke of Wellington) arrived in Portugal to command British troops. Outnumbered by the French, he withdrew to Lisbon, the capital, behind strong lines of defence. The countryside round about was devastated on Wellington's orders and when the French arrived to besiege Lisbon they found neither food nor shelter. Over the next two years the French were gradually worn down, and in March 1811 the French commander Massena gave his weak and hungry men the order to retreat.

Harassed all the way by Wellington's army, the French withdrew across Spain. They were finally defeated at the Battle of Vitoria, on 21 June 1813.

Later that year, the British invaded France. On 10 April, 1814 they captured Toulouse. It was an unnecessary battle since, on 6 April 1814, Napoleon had abdicated — though the news had not reached Wellington.

Napoleon fights on

Meanwhile, Russia, Prussia, Sweden and Britain had formed a coalition against Napoleon. Their combined armies conducted a campaign in central Germany against the French through the summer of 1813. But Napoleon's resources were declining while those of the Allies (now joined by Austria) grew stronger. Between 16 and 19 October, the French were routed at Leipzig and the Allies closed in on France. On 11 April 1814, Napoleon surrendered. The Allies exiled him on the Mediterranean island of Elba.

Waterloo

In March 1815 Napoleon got away from Elba and returned to France. Amazingly, he raised yet another army. On 18 June, the Allies under Wellington defeated him at the Battle of Waterloo.

The victors imprisoned Napoleon on St Helena, an island in the South Atlantic so remote that escape was impossible. He died there in 1821.

The Wars of the Early 19th Century and After

The War of 1812

Opposing sides United States v Britain.
Causes 1. British (at war with
 France) interfered with US trade with
 France. 2. US aim to seize Canada.
Battlegrounds Canada, eastern United
 States, Atlantic Ocean.
Main events 1812 British fleet blockades
 coast of USA while war lasts and lands
 raiding parties to burn and destroy. June:
 US invasion of Canada fails. August:
 British capture Detroit. 1813 September:
 US force recaptures Detroit. Another US
 invasion of Canada fails. US wins naval
 battle on Lake Erie. 1814 July: British
 lose Battle of Chippewa but besiege
 Americans in Fort Erie. August/
 September: British raiders occupy
 Washington, burn public buildings and
 bombard Baltimore. September: British
 invasion of US from Montreal halted
 after losing Battle of Plattsburg. Battle of
 Lake Champlain. US defeat British.
 Danger of invasion from Canada ended.
 December: Treaty of Ghent ends war.

1815 January: Battle of New Orleans.
 Fought because news of peace had not
 yet reached America. Americans beat off
 British attack.
Outcome Both sides return captured
 territory. End of US attempt to conquer
 Canada.

The United States-Mexican War

Opposing sides United States v Mexico.
Causes 1. Mexico objects to US
 annexation of Texas. 2. US aim to gain
 Mexican territories in far southwest.
Leaders US: Generals Zachary Taylor and
 Winfield Scott v Mexico: President
 Santa Anna.
Battlegrounds California, New Mexico,
 Texas, Mexico.
Main events 1. Northern Campaign: 1846
 May: US force under Zachary Taylor
 invades Mexico. September: Taylor
 captures Monterey (Mexico). 1847
 February: Taylor wins Battle of Buena
 Vista. Mexicans under Santa Anna

retreat. End of Northern Campaign.
2. Western Campaign. 1846 June: US
 expedition lands on Californian coast
 and occupies Monterey. 1847 January:
 Battle of San Gabriel. End of Mexican
 resistance.
3. Campaign in Central Mexico: 1847
 March: Winfield Scott heads US
 expedition which lands from the sea and
 captures Vera Cruz. April: Scott routs
 Mexicans under Santa Anna at Cerro
 Gordo. September: Scott's force captures
 Mexico City. 1848 February: Peace
 Treaty of Guadalupe Hidalgo.
Outcome US gains vast new territories in
 southwest, including California, Nevada
 and Utah.

The Crimean War

Opposing sides Russia v France, Britain,
 Turkey and Sardinia.
Causes Russia attacks Turkey.
 Britain and France fear extension of

*The Mexican War of 1846-1847 resulted
in a vast territory being given up to the
United States. The Mexicans did not really
stand a chance. In many battles they
were superior in numbers, but their troops
were poorly trained, and ill-equipped.*

*Florence Nightingale brought not just
comfort to the wounded soldiers of the
Crimean War. She revolutionized
nursing practice, and pressured the
military to increase provisions and
improve conditions.*

Russian power and go to Turkey's aid.

Leaders Russia: Menshikov and
Gorchakov v Allies: Raglan, Lucan and
Saint-Arnaud.

Battleground Crimean peninsula in Black
Sea (in present-day Ukraine).

Main events 1853 Russia and Turkey at
war. Russia destroys Turkish fleet at
Sinope. 1854 March: France and Britain
declare war. September: Franco-British
force lands in Crimea. Wins Battle of the
Alma and besieges great Russian naval
base of Sevastopol. October: Allied
victory at Battle of Balaklava (Charge of
the Light Brigade). November: Allies
withstand Russian attack and win Battle
of Inkerman. 1854 November-1855
March: Bitter Russian winter. British
unprepared. Short of food and warm
clothing. Medical facilities appalling.
Thousands die until Florence Nightingale
organizes hospitals and proper medical
attention at Scutari. 1855 February:
Sardinian troops join Allies. September:
Allies capture Sevastopol. 1856 March:
Congress and subsequent Treaty of Paris
end war.

Outcome Russia hands back Turkish
territory. British soldiers' conditions
greatly improved.

The Indian Mutiny

Opposing sides British forces stationed in
India and Indians who stayed loyal to
them v mutinous Indian troops.

Causes 1. Indians deeply offended by
reforms imposed by arrogant British
rulers. 2. Indians refuse to use new rifle
cartridges greased with fat of animals
they hold sacred.

Leaders British commanders: John and
Henry Lawrence, Henry Havelock and
Colin Campbell v Indian Nana Sahib
and Tantia Topi.

Battleground Northern India.

Main events 1857 May: Meerut. Indian
troops mutiny and murder British
soldiers and civilians. They flee to Delhi
where Indian garrison troops join rebels.
Together, they massacre all British who
cannot escape. June: Mutiny spreads.
60,000 rebels besiege British in Lucknow.

At Cawnpore, mutineers offer safe
conduct to trapped British then slaughter
them. September: British recapture Delhi.
British force breaks through rebels at
Lucknow but is then itself besieged.
November: British relieve Lucknow and
defeat rebels. 1858 June: Battle of
Gwalior. British crush rebels with great
brutality. End of mutiny.

Outcome East India Company abolished.
Atrocities sour Indo-British relations.

The Austro-Prussian War

Opposing sides Prussia v Austria and states
of South Germany.

Causes Rivalry between Austria and
Prussia over leadership of Germany.

Battleground Germany and Bohemia.

Main events 1866 June: Prussians attack
on broad front. They invade Hanover,
Silesia and Saxony. Prussians defeat
Hanoverian army. They advance down
the River Elbe and try to trap the Aus-
trians. July: Battle of Sadowa (or
Königgrätz). Prussian victory. August:
Treaty of Prague ends war.

Outcome Austria excluded from German
affairs. North German states join in a
confederation and Prussia becomes their
leader. Prussia now the undisputed leader
of Germany.

The War of Italian Independence

Opposing sides Austro-Hungarian Empire
v Italian patriots.

Causes Italians aim to drive out the
Austrians and create a free and
independent Italy.

Leaders Italians: Count Camillo Cavour,
prime minister of Piedmont. Giuseppe
Garibaldi, guerrilla leader.

Battlegrounds Sicily and Italy.

Main events 1859 Small Italian kingdom
of Piedmont allied with France wins war
against Austria. (Suffering of wounded at
Battle of Solferino inspires foundation of
Red Cross movement.) War confirms
Piedmont as leading state in Italy. 1860
May-July: Garibaldi invades and
occupies Sicily. August: Garibaldi lands
in Italy. September: He captures Naples.
Piedmontese invade Papal States and
march south to link up with Garibaldi.
1861 February: Combined force captures
last Neapolitan stronghold at Gaeta.
March: Kingdom of Italy proclaimed.
(Rome and Venice remain outside.) 1866
June: Italy joins Prussia in war against
Austria. October: Italy gains Venice at
Treaty of Vienna. 1870 September:
Italian army occupies Rome.

Outcome Italy united and independent.

*Garibaldi and his redshirts land in Sicily
and claim the island for the newly
established Kingdom of Italy. Garibaldi
went from there to the mainland, where
he captured Naples.*

The American Civil War

A divided land

By the year 1860, the question of slavery threatened to split the United States apart. In the North, the population was increasing rapidly. Northern cities were expanding and trade and industry were fast replacing farming as the main source of profitable cotton-growing. And if slavery were ended, the privileged and gracious way of life the Southerners prized so much would be in peril.

The issue of slavery

The future of slavery was threatened by the growth of the throughout the whole country.

In 1860, Abraham Lincoln was elected president. Lincoln opposed the spread of slavery to the new states and to the Southerners his election was the last straw. They feared that their battle to extend slavery to the new states was as good as

wealth. The Southern states had changed little. They were still a rural area where the main crop was cotton, grown on huge plantations by black slave workers. Southerners were determined to maintain slavery. Slave labour was cheap and cheap labour was essential to United States. New states formed out of the empty lands of the West were lining up to join the Union. Their policies would settle the fate of slavery. If the new states opposed slavery the anti-slavers would dominate both Congress and Senate and pass laws ending slavery lost. Within a year, eleven southern states had opted to leave the Union. They formed a Confederacy which was in effect a breakaway nation.

Lincoln tried to avert a conflict by offering to allow the states which maintained slavery to keep it. At the same time he

The United States on the eve of the Civil War. Nebraska and Kansas were part of a huge area bought from France in the 1803 Louisiana Purchase. Texas had won its independence from Mexico in 1836, and become a state in 1845. California and New Mexico were taken over in 1848.

emphasized that no state had the right to weaken the Union as a whole by leaving it.

The war begins

On 12 April 1861, Confederate troops opened fire on the Federal (Union) garrison of Fort Sumter in Charleston Harbour. Lincoln promptly ordered a blockade of Confederate ports and called for volunteers to join the Federal Army. The ablest American soldier of the time was the Southerner Robert E. Lee. Both sides offered him high command in their forces. Lee felt his loyalty lay with the South and chose to accept the Confederate command. Meanwhile the Confederate States had elected Jefferson Davis as their president.

The opening battles

The first major battle of the war was fought on 21 July 1861, at Bull Run, on the Potomac River. After hours of hard fighting, the Union troops fled, leaving the nearby capital, Washington, undefended. However, the Southerners were too exhausted to follow up their victory. In the West, the Union was more successful. Federal forces under Brigadier-General Ulysses S. Grant won control of the state of Kentucky.

Shiloh

The Union commanders now tried, unsuccessfully, to split the Confederacy by occupying the Mississippi valley. On 6 April, 1862, Grant's Union army defeated the Confederates at Shiloh. Nearly a quarter

the harbour. She sank two of them and drove the others ashore while Union cannon balls bounced harmlessly off her armour. When the *Merrimack* sailed out to finish off the remaining Union ships the next morning, she found the *Monitor* waiting for her. The two iron-clad ships exchanged fire, but neither was able to penetrate the armour plating of the other. The contest ended in stalemate, but it had changed sea warfare for ever. After the *Merrimack* and the *Monitor* wooden warships were obsolete.

of the soldiers engaged were killed or wounded. The carnage at Shiloh was the first indication of the terrible slaughter to come.

The war at sea

The Civil War saw the world's first battle between armour-plated warships. The Confederates salvaged a wooden steam freighter called the *Merrimack* and sheathed it in thick iron plates. In reply, the Union built a ship entirely of iron named the *Monitor*.

On 8 March 1862, the *Merrimack* steamed out of Norfolk, Virginia, towards the five wooden Union ships blockading

General Grant was the best Union general of the Civil War. He looked unimpressive and he was rumoured to have a drink problem, but he led his troops to victory. Later he was elected President of the United States, but was less successful in government.

The first battle between two ironclads, the Merrimack *and the* Monitor, *was inconclusive. Neither vessel could pierce the other's armour. It proved that the wooden-hulled warship had seen its day.*

Map: Most of the fighting in the east took place in Virginia. Richmond was the Confederate capital. General McClellan thought that he could capture the city and finish the war, but General Lee and Stonewall Jackson outmanoeuvred him.

The war in the East

In December 1861, George B. McClellan was appointed general-in-chief of the Union armies. Urged on by Lincoln, who wanted a quick end to the war, he advanced against the Confederate capital at Richmond.

At the end of May 1862, he beat off an ill-organized Confederate attack at the Battle of Fair Oaks (Seven Pines). This defeat helped the South. Robert E. Lee replaced the Southern commander, who had been badly wounded in the battle.

Lee planned a campaign to keep the Federal forces divided by preventing the Union troops in Washington joining up with McClellan's army near Richmond. First he sent General 'Stonewall' Jackson ('Stonewall' because of his steadiness in battle) to create a diversion in the Shenandoah valley. In a month-long campaign, Jackson tied down large Union forces before rejoining Lee in late June. On 29-30 August, near Washington, Lee's army attacked a Union force under Major-General John Pope. The result was the Second Battle of Bull Run (Second Manassas). The Union army was soundly defeated and withdrew to Washington.

Lee now prepared to invade the North. His objective was

partly political. He and President Davis believed that a successful invasion might encourage France and Britain to recognize the Confederacy and even give it aid.

General Lee was admired by both sides for his character, courage and military expertise. He rode his horse Traveller throughout the war, and to the surrender. He told his followers 'to abandon local hatreds and make your sons Americans'.

Stonewall Jackson was General Lee's most able subordinate. His death, after he was accidentally wounded by his own men, was a tragedy for Lee who believed he would have won Gettysburg with Jackson in command.

General McClellan was a cautious man, loath to risk his soldiers' lives, but an inspiring leader who kept the discipline and morale of his troops high.

Antietam

Lee's plans fell into the hands of General McClellan, the Union commander, but he moved too slowly to take full advantage of his good fortune. Lee managed to concentrate his forces at Antietam Creek (Sharpsburg) before McClellan struck, on 17 September. It was the bloodiest single day's fighting of the war; both sides lost over 12,000 men. Lee held his ground, but his losses forced him to retreat and abandon the planned invasion.

Lincoln's patience finally ran out when McClellan failed to pursue Lee's army. Major-General Ambrose E. Burnside was given command, but resigned after losing the Battle of Fredericksburg against Lee on 13 December.

Chancellorsville

Burnside's successor, 'Fighting Joe' Hooker, planned to encircle Lee's position at Fredericksburg, but Lee's scouts made him well aware of Hooker's intentions. At Chancellorsville,

between 1 and 6 May 1863, Lee's army won a tremendous victory over an enemy nearly twice its size. But Lee lost the man he could least afford to spare. Stonewall Jackson was wounded and died shortly after the battle.

The Gettysburg Campaign

In mid-1863, Lee launched his second invasion of the North. On 30 June, Union and Confederate troops met by accident near Gettysburg, Pennsylvania. The unexpected clash developed into the war's biggest battle.

Fighting began in earnest on 1 July, but the first two days were indecisive. On 3 July, Lee ordered a frontal assault on the Union troops lining Cemetery

Clara Barton was known as the 'angel of the battlefields'. Though she had neither medical nor military training, she organized the nursing of wounded Union soldiers throughout the war, often exposing herself to great personal danger and hardship.

Pickett's charge at the Battle of Gettysburg. Following a hat held high, 15,000 Confederate soldiers marched into a hail of Union fire. Less than a thousand men reached their target. Those who did fought hand to hand before surrendering, but most retreated.

Hill. Covered by an immense artillery bombardment, 15,000 Confederate soldiers advanced on the Union line through violent defensive fire. The few that reached the enemy line were thrown back. The attack had failed and Lee was forced to retreat. Altogether, the Battle of Gettysburg cost the two sides over 50,000 casualties.

The loss of Vicksburg
Vicksburg was a Confederate stronghold on the Mississippi. The town linked the eastern and western states of the Confederacy and controlled the routes through the Mississippi valley. Since May 1863, Vicksburg had been besieged by a Union army under General Grant. On 4 July, the day after Lee's defeat at Gettysburg, Vicksburg surrendered.

The loss of Vicksburg was a mortal blow to the Confederates. Its fall gave the Union control of the entire Mississippi valley and split the Confederacy in two.

Chickamauga – 'River of Death'
The centre of the railway system of the South was Chattanooga, Tennessee. In September 1863, the Confederates under General Braxton Bragg, abandoned it to avoid being cut off by a Federal army. To

From Lincoln's Gettysburg Address
'. . . we here highly resolve that these dead shall not have died in vain – that this nation, under God, shall have a new birth of freedom – and that government of the people, by the people, for the people, shall not perish from the earth.'
19 November 1863

Map: The capture of the Confederate stronghold of Vicksburg gave the North complete control of the Mississippi, and spilt the South in two.

regain this vital rail junction, President Davis ordered fresh troops to be rushed by rail to join Bragg's force. The armies met at Chickamauga Creek on 19 September. After two days of heavy fighting, the Union forces withdrew to Chattanooga, where they were besieged by the Confederates.

In October, General Grant became overall commander of Union forces in the West. Reinforced by General William T Sherman's army he overwhelmed the Confederates in the Battle of Chattanooga on 24-25 November.

The Union closes in

Grant, promoted general-in-chief of all the Union armies, now planned a two-pronged attack on the Confederacy to bring a quick end to the war. He himself would march on Richmond, the Confederate capital, while another army under

Sherman struck deep into enemy territory towards Atlanta.

Lee attempted to bar Grant's march in the dense thickets of an area called the Wilderness. Both sides lost heavily in two days of furious, confused fighting, but, undeterred, Grant marched on towards Richmond. Lee now showed what a brilliant general he was. In a series of actions ending in the Battle of Cold Harbor, 3-12 June, he

inflicted severe casualties on the Union forces. However, the Union's resources of men and material were vast compared to those of the Confederacy. Grant knew he could make good his losses and pressed on. He now planned to cut Richmond's life-line at Petersburg, a rail junction through which passed all supplies for the capital. The Union attack on Petersburg's defences failed and Grant settled down to cut off

the city and starve out its defenders.

Sherman's march

In the meantime, on 2 September, Sherman's Union army had captured Atlanta. From there, Sherman set out to march through Georgia to the sea. His troops spread terror as they went, for they created a corridor of destruction, 80 km (50 miles) wide, as they passed. On 21 December, they reached the coast and captured Savannah. What remained of the Confederacy was now cut in two.

Chatanooga was defended by a Confederate army under General Bragg. In October 1863 General Grant launched an attack on Lookout Mountain that came to be known as the 'battle above the clouds'. The defending Confederates were beaten by vastly superior numbers.

William T Sherman had not been a great success in civilian life. His military achievements were outstanding, though he was thought by many to be unnecessarily ruthless.

Map: General Sherman, advancing through Georgia, cut a swathe of death and destruction, once more dividing the South. He reached Savannah, on the coast, in December, and then marched north through the Carolinas.

The South surrenders

The Confederacy was doomed. Lee was forced to abandon Petersburg and his army was surrounded. He surrendered at Appomattox, Virginia, on 9 April 1865, and by the end of May all other Confederate forces had laid down their arms.

Lincoln did not live to enjoy the Union's victory. On 14 April, he was shot and killed by a Southerner, John Wilkes Booth.

Results of the war

The Civil War saved the United States from breaking up and slavery was abolished. Over 600,000 Americans were killed in the conflict. More lost their lives then than in either of the two world wars of the 20th century. The South was ruined by the war and the bitterness it caused poisoned American life for generations to come.

A lasting peace

'With malice toward none; with charity for all; with firmness in the right, as God gives us to see the right, let us strive on to the finish of the work we are in; to bind up the nation's wounds; to care for him who shall have borne the battle, and for his widow and his orphan – to do all which may achieve and cherish a just, and a lasting peace, among ourselves, and with all nations.'

From Lincoln's second
inaugural speech,
4 March 1865.

Sherman knew that the way to defeat the South was to cripple its economy. Rather than fighting pitched battles, he waged war on the entire civilian population, first cutting railway communications, then destroying homes, villages, towns and farms.

General Grant shakes hands with General Lee after the signing of the surrender document. Lee was as dignified as always. Grant had to apologise to him for his own unkempt appearance. He had come straight from the battlefield.

The Wars of the Late 19th Century and After

The Franco-Prussian War

Opposing sides France v Germany led by Prussia.

Causes Bad relations between France and Prussia made war inevitable. Immediate cause – Prussian attempt to place a German prince on the Spanish throne.

Leaders France: Emperor Napoleon III v Prussia: Chancellor Bismarck.

Battlegrounds Franco-German border and northeast France.

Main events 1870 August: French lose series of minor battles. German army shows its superiority. September: French routed at Battle of Sedan. Napoleon surrenders. German army advances on Paris. French people prepare to defend Paris and rally to rescue France. They throw out Emperor Napoleon and found a republic. Germans besiege Paris. October-December: Widespread fighting as French try to relieve Paris. 1871 January: Major French defeats at Le Mans and Belfort, but fortress city of Belfort still holds out. Paris surrenders. May: Treaty of Frankfurt ends war. French lose Alsace and part of Lorraine to Germany and pay the cost of the war (5 billion francs).

Outcome Germany united under Prussian leadership and now the most powerful state in Europe.

The Spanish-American War

Opposing sides Spain v United States.

Causes of war 1. US public outraged by Spanish cruelty in putting down a revolt in Cuba, then a Spanish colony. 2. Spain blamed when US battleship *Maine* mysteriously blows up in Havana harbour.

Battlegrounds Philippines, Cuba, Puerto Rico.

Main events 1898 April: US declares war. 1. War in the Pacific. April: US naval squadron under Commodore Dewey sails

to attack Spanish colony of the Philippines. May: Dewey wins Battle of Manila Bay. June: US expedition arrives from San Francisco and lands near Manila. August: Spaniards in Philippines surrender.

2. War in the Caribbean: 1898 May: US fleet blockades Cuba. June: US military expedition lands in Cuba. July: It wins battles of San Juan and El Caney. At sea, US ships destroy Spanish fleet at Battle of Santiago Bay. Spaniards on Cuba surrender. July: US troops land on Puerto Rico and overwhelm Spanish garrison. December: Peace signed at Treaty of Paris.

Outcome Cuba becomes independent. US gains Puerto Rico, and the Pacific island of Guam. US buys the Philippines for $20 million.

The Boer War

Opposing sides Britain v Boers (descendants of original Dutch settlers in South Africa).

Causes Long-term conflict between Boers and British. 1899 British prepare to seize the Transvaal Republic, the Boers' homeland. Boers strike while British are still gathering an invasion force.

Major figures Boers: Cronjé, Botha v British: Buller, Baden-Powell, Roberts.

Battleground South Africa.

Main events 1899 October: Boers attack. They besiege Mafeking (Baden-Powell), Kimberley and Ladysmith. British try to relieve them and suffer heavy losses at battles of Laing's Nek, Colenso and Magersfontein. British commander Buller replaced by Roberts. 1900 Roberts reorganizes British forces. February: British relieve Kimberley and Ladysmith. March: Fresh British troops arrive. May: Mafeking freed. British invade Transvaal. June: Boer capital Pretoria captured. Boers begin guerrilla war. Eventually, harsh British measures force them to give in. 1902 May: Treaty of Vereeniging ends war. Generous terms help Boers to accept British rule.

Outcome 1907 Boers given self-government.

Otto von Bismarck came from a wealthy Prussian family. He was a highly skilled military strategist, politician and diplomat. He united the German states into one empire. Prior to the Franco-Prussian War he fought and defeated Denmark (1864) and Austria (1866).

*The battleship **Maine** had been sent to Havana to protect American citizens in Cuba, after Spain granted the island partial self-government. An explosion blew up the ship shortly after it arrived. It was probably an accident but the American public blamed Spain.*

The Boxer Rising

Opposing sides Foreigners (mainly British, German, Russian, American and French) living in China v Members of Chinese secret society 'Society of Harmonious Fists' (The Boxers).

Causes Young, patriotic Chinese resent greed and arrogance of foreign community. They band together to drive foreigners out.

Battleground Northern China.

Main events 1900 Boxers attack foreign missionaries, workers and merchants. Chinese government secretly supports them. June: Small force (mainly British) lands to protect foreigners. Boxers drive them back to ships. Mobs murder German minister in Peking (Beijing) and besiege foreign embassies. Foreign powers assemble mixed force to go to the rescue. July: Relief force 18,700 strong captures Tientsin. August: It marches on Peking. City is captured and looted by foreign troops. They destroy Chinese towns and villages nearby as punishment. September: Foreign powers force China to pay $740 million compensation for losses due to Boxer action.

Outcome Anti-foreign feeling grows in China. Many young Chinese join republican movement led by Sun Yat-sen.

The Russo-Japanese War

Opposing sides Russia v Japan.

Causes Japan and Russia rivals for power in Manchuria and Korea. Japanese plan to drive Russians out.

Battlegrounds Manchuria, Korea and seas around.

Main events 1904 8 February: Surprise Japanese attack on Russian ships in Port Arthur, key Russian naval base in Manchuria. 10 February: War declared.
1. Land Campaign 1904 February: Japanese land in Korea. April: They defeat Russians at the Yalu River and advance to attack Port Arthur (Lüshun) from the land. May: Siege of Port Arthur begins. 1905 January: Port Arthur surrenders. Siege costs Japanese 59,000 casualties. Russian losses, 39,000. March: Japanese victory at Battle of Mukden is last major land battle.
2. Action at sea 1904 October: Russian Baltic fleet sets off to sail halfway round the world to fight Japan. Fires on British fishing boats in North Sea and almost causes war with Britain. 1905 May: Battle of Tsushima. Japanese destroy Russian Baltic fleet. 1905 September: Treaty of Portsmouth ends war.

Outcome Russia gives up Port Arthur and gets out of Manchuria. Japan recognized as dominant power in Korea.

First Balkan War

Opposing sides Turkey v Balkan League (Bulgaria, Serbia, Greece and Montenegro).

Causes Balkan League aims to drive Turks out of Europe and seize Turkish possessions in Balkans.

Battlegrounds Last fragments of Turkey's empire in the Balkans; Macedonia and Thrace.

Main events 1912 October: League forces invade Turkish territory. November: Serbs win Battle of Monastir. Both Greeks and Bulgars want Salonika, but Greeks arrive first and capture it. December: League forces try but fail to take Constantinople. 1913 May: Major European powers intervene to stop the fighting and prevent it developing into a general European war. Treaty of London ends war.

Outcome Turkey keeps Gallipoli but loses remaining Balkan territories to her enemies. They fall out among themselves over division of the spoils. New state of Albania created.

The Second Balkan War

Opposing sides Bulgaria v Greece and Serbia, joined later by Romania and Turkey.

Causes Bulgaria dissatisfied by settlement made after First Balkan War. Serbs refuse to hand over territory where majority of the people are Bulgarian. Bulgaria determined to take this land by force.

Battlegrounds Serbia, Bulgaria.

Main events 1913 May: Bulgarians launch surprise attacks against the Serbs and their Greek allies. July: Both attacks halted. Romania and Turkey take advantage of Bulgaria's plight to enter war against her. Bulgaria forced to surrender. August: Treaty of Bucharest ends war.

Outcome Bulgaria loses all gains made in First Balkan War. Balkans remain a dangerously unstable area and trigger outbreak of World War I.

In 1900 a British force landed in Kowloon (Hong Kong) in an effort to protect foreigners who were being persecuted by Boxers who beseiged their embassies.

World War I

The immediate cause of war was rivalry in the Balkans between Austria-Hungary and Russia. In June 1914, in Sarajevo, a Serbian nationalist assassinated the heir to the throne of Austria-Hungary. The Austrians blamed the Serbian government for the murder and declared war on Serbia. Serbia's ally Russia promptly declared war on Austria. Germany was allied to Austria. She declared war on Russia and on Russia's ally, France. On 3 August, German armies invaded Belgium in

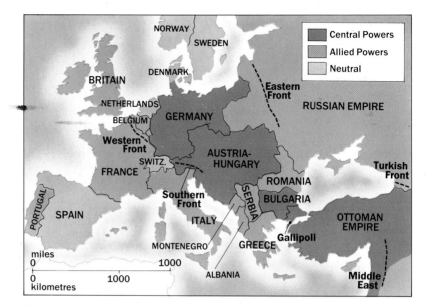

The 19-year-old Serbian student Gavrilo Princip opposed Austrian rule of Bosnia, which wanted to join up with Serbia. When the heir to the Austrian throne, Archduke Franz Ferdinand, visited Sarajevo, Princip shot him and his wife dead, triggering the outbreak of war.

Map: The Central Powers, Germany and Austria-Hungary, were encircled by the main Allied Powers, France, Britain and Russia.

Turkey joined the Central Powers in the first days of the war. In October, the Turkish navy bombarded several of Russia's Black Sea ports and Russia asked her French and British allies for help.

The Allies fatally underestimated the Turks. In March 1915, an Anglo-French fleet sailed to Russia's aid. It was driven off by Turkish guns overlooking the Dardanelles, the straits which led into the Black Sea.

In April, a mixed British and British Empire force attempted to capture Gallipoli, a rocky peninsula commanding the entrance to the Dardanelles. The Turks hung on grimly and in January 1916, after seven months of savage trench warfare, the British withdrew. The campaign had cost them over 200,000 casualties.

order to attack France along the undefended Franco-Belgian frontier. Britain was committed to defend Belgium and immediately declared war on Germany. By mid-August 1914 virtually the whole of the continent was at war. On one side were the Allied Powers led by France, Britain and Russia. On the other were

Paris, but the French Army aided by a small British contingent forced them to retreat to a line of defensive trenches along the River Aisne. The Allies dug a similar trench network facing the Germans. Soon, trenches stretched unbroken from the Swiss border to the English Channel.

the Central Powers led by Germany and Austria-Hungary.

Trench warfare begins
The Germans planned a quick strike to knock France out of the war. They got close to

Four years of carnage followed as the opposing armies shelled, machine-gunned and gassed each other in futile attempts to break through the other's defences. Men lived, fought and died in nightmare conditions.

Wilhelm II (left), was emperor of Germany from 1888 to 1918. Joseph Joffre (centre) was Supreme Allied Commander from 1914 to 1916, and later Marshal of France. Douglas Haig (right) was British commander-in-chief during the second half of the war.

Trenches were cold, wet and unhealthy. In front of them were thickets of barbed wire dotted with machine-gun posts, directed across a stretch of no man's land to the enemy trenches. Behind the trenches were living quarters, first-aid stations and supply depots.

In 1915 a new German weapon arrived on the battlefield at Ypres in the shape of a billowing greenish-yellow cloud. It was poisonous chlorine gas. At first it terrified the troops, but when gas masks proved effective it became only a nuisance, and both sides used it.

The Russian Revolution

The Russians did not win the war, but they prevented the Allies from losing it. At critical times in the West, Russian attacks on Germany's eastern frontiers drew huge numbers of German troops away from the Western Front.

But Russia suffered huge casualties. In 1916 alone, over a million Russian soldiers were taken prisoner by the Germans. An exceptionally severe winter followed. In Russia, food and fuel were rationed, and in March 1917 (February in the old Russian calendar), workers in Petrograd (now St Petersburg) rioted. Troops sent to restore order joined the rioters and the unrest spread to other cities.

The revolt became a revolution. By November (October) left-wing Socialists called

Bolsheviks had gained power. Led by Trotsky and Lenin, their first aim was to end the war. They signed peace with Germany on 3 March 1918.

War at sea

At sea, the war was fought chiefly between Britain and Germany. The greatest battle took place in the North Sea, off Jutland, in May 1916. The British lost more ships than the Germans, but the German Grand Fleet withdrew to its home ports after the action was over. It failed to come out again for the rest of the war.

The pilot of a single-seat fighter had to line his plane up behind the enemy and then fire the machine gun fixed to its nose. Here a Sopwith F1 Camel hits its target while a Fokker Dr.1 triplane gets out of the way.

A German 420mm howitzer bombards the French at Verdun. Over a thousand French and British heavy guns on a 40-kilometre front poured 1,738,000 shells onto the German trenches before the Battle of the Somme.

The U-boat menace

German submarines almost starved Britain into defeat. In early 1917, in the space of three months, German U-boats sank 470 merchant ships bringing vital supplies to Britain. Only by grouping merchant ships into convoys and by developing more effective counter-measures were the British able to contain the submarine menace.

War in the air

The aircraft of 1914 were slow, unreliable and unarmed. They were used mainly for observing enemy troop movements. But the needs of war stimulated rapid advances in aircraft design. By the end of the conflict, air battles and machine-gunning of the trenches had became a regular feature of warfare.

Germany had led the world before the war in airship design. Called 'Zeppelins' after their inventor, these huge craft pioneered the bombing of civilian targets far from the battle-fronts. Between 1915 and 1917, Zeppelins dropped 6,000 tonnes of bombs on British cities.

Tank warfare

Tanks were developed to end trench warfare. First used in a minor battle on the Somme in 1916, they could crush barbed wire, cross trenches and withstand machine-gun fire. At Cambrai, in November 1917, 476 tanks forced the German lines back 10,000 metres, proving the tank's war-winning potential.

The Italian Front

Italy entered the war on the Allied side in 1915, claiming territory occupied by her former ally, Austria. The battle-front lay along the frontier between the two countries in the Alps. A two-year stalemate was broken in October 1917 when the Austrians defeated the Italians at Caporetto and drove them back to the River Piave. A year later, an Italian army with Allied reinforcements routed the Austrians at Vittorio Veneto a week before the war ended. Italy also took the Adriatic port of Trieste.

The first tanks rolled into battle on the Somme in 1916. In 1917, tanks like this 25-tonne Mark IV scored a spectacular success at Cambrai.

War in the desert

Control of the Middle East was essential to Britain. The region commanded vital sea routes and was the source of the oil Britain needed to keep her war effort going. But the Turkish empire straddled the area, and when Turkey joined the Central Powers, war in the Middle East became inevitable.

In late 1914, Anglo-Indian troops occupied Basra and made it their base for protecting the oil fields of Mesopotamia. Another Allied force repulsed a Turkish push towards the Suez Canal and advanced north into Palestine. But the Allied advance was itself turned into a retreat, and in April 1916 the Turks captured the town of Kut al-Amara with its Allied garrison.

The following year, led by a new commander, General Allenby, and with the support of the Arabs who had risen against Turkish rule, Allied troops recaptured Kut. They followed this by taking Baghdad and entering Jerusalem. The entire Middle East had come under Allied control by the end of the war in November 1918.

The Western Front

The position of the trench-lines on the Western Front hardly changed in the first four years of the war. The grim, inhuman struggle there went on without ceasing.

In 1915, the Germans used poison gas as a surprise terror

weapon. The Allied line held, but from then onwards, poison gas was used by both sides.

1916 was a year of almost unbroken slaughter. A German attempt to exterminate the French army at Verdun in 1916 failed, but at the expense of enormous losses on both sides. At the same time, the British were losing more than half a million men in the Battle of the Somme.

America joins the war

In February 1917, German U-boats were ordered to sink on sight and without warning all ships trading with Britain. Several American vessels were lost in this way and the United States, in response to public

The aftermath of battle. In 1917 the 3rd Battle of Ypres was fought in Belgium. Heavy rain turned the battlefield into a swamp. In five months the Allies advanced less than five miles but lost almost a quarter of a million men.

Philippe Pétain (left) was a hero to the French because of his unyielding defence of Verdun. T.E. Lawrence (centre) led Arab guerrilla fighters against the Turks. United States president Woodrow Wilson (right) kept America out of the war until April 1917.

opinion, declared war on Germany on 6 April.

The Germans now realized their one remaining chance of victory was to defeat the British and French before thousands of fresh American troops could arrive in Europe. Beginning in March 1918, they launched a series of offensives, but failed to break the Allied line. In May the Americans joined the final onslaught which overwhelmed the German army. An Armistice to end the fighting was signed on 11 November 1918.

The peace that led to war

The Treaty of Versailles which formally ended the war was signed in June 1919. It treated Germany harshly. She lost 13 per cent of her pre-war territory. Her colonies were divided among the Allies and she was forced to pay a gigantic fine for causing the war. The Allies also barred Germany from the League of Nations, the organization set up to keep peace in the postwar world.

The treaty caused lasting bitterness in Germany. As she recovered from the war, Germany became increasingly hostile towards the League and its members. The major powers were divided into two armed camps and, in 1939, after twenty years of uneasy peace, the world again was plunged into war by Germany's ambition.

The Yanks are coming! The arrival of the Americans put new heart into the Allies. The Germans made an effort to finish off the exhausted British and French before millions of fresh troops arrived, but failed.

The Russian Revolution

The origins of revolt

In early 1905, in St Petersburg, the capital of Russia, starving workers went on strike to protest at the conditions under which they lived. On Sunday 22 January, government troops fired on workers marching towards the Winter Palace of the Russian tsar.

The affair of 'Bloody Sunday' sparked off widespread unrest. In October, a nationwide strike brought all Russia to a halt. Representatives of the strikers set up a Soviet or workers' council which for a short while seemed likely to rule the country. Tsar Nicholas now took action to end the disorder. He agreed to a series of minor reforms including the creation of an elected Duma, or parliament. The Duma had no real power. Duma members could only advise the tsar and elections to it were managed so as to exclude everyone likely to be a nuisance to the authorities.

Marx and Lenin

One of the government's most dangerous opponents was the writer Lenin. In 1900, after years of imprisonment by the tsar's secret police, he left Russia. He settled eventually in Switzerland and from there published a stream of newspapers and pamphlets preaching the doctrines of the German revolutionary philosopher Karl Marx. He became accepted as the leader of the 'Bolsheviks', the most extreme opponents of the government of the tsar.

Tsar Nicholas II and Empress Alexandra were the last reigning representatives of the House of Romanov which ruled Russia for 300 years.

Bloody Sunday: 22 January 1905. A procession of striking workers, 200,000 strong, followed Father Gapon through the snowy streets to the Winter Palace to appeal to the tsar. They were mown down by rifle fire.

In 1914, Russia entered the war against Germany and Austria-Hungary. By late 1916, over five million of Russia's brave but poorly armed soldiers had been killed, wounded or captured.

The winter of 1916-1917 was exceptionally severe. Urgently needed food and fuel failed to reach the cities because the railways were used entirely for the transport of war supplies. The people were cold and starving, but the tsar's government did nothing to help them.

In March 1917, the angry workers of Petrograd (now St Petersburg) rioted in protest. Troops sent to suppress the disorder joined the rioters and the revolt spread. The tsar tried to dismiss the Duma, but its members defied him and on March 14 they elected a Provisional Government. The revolt had become a revolution. The next day the tsar abdicated.

Enter Lenin

In Switzerland, Lenin could only watch these events from afar. But the Germans sent him back to Russia in secret, hoping that he would cause a great deal of trouble once he arrived there. He turned up in Petrograd on 16 April 1917, and was greeted as a hero.

Meanwhile, the Provisional Government set up by the Duma was introducing reforms.

Karl Marx did not live to see the Revolution that his works inspired. According to his theory of Communism, private property would be abolished and the state would become unnecessary.

Waving the red flag, Russian soldiers at the front cheer the news that the tsar has been overthrown. By commanding a losing army, Nicholas had added further proof of his incompetence.

Alexander Kerensky was briefly leader of the Provisional Government. Though he was originally sympathetic to the Bolsheviks, he fled after failing to prevent the Bolsheviks seizing power. He spent the rest of his life in the United States.

The civil war

The Bolsheviks, now calling themselves Communists, met with widespread opposition. Britain, France and other western nations, who were anxious to stamp out Communism at source before it spread throughout the world, supported the anti-Communists with troops and supplies. Civil war raged until 1922, when the Communist Red Army, brilliantly organized by Trotsky, finally defeated the enemy and cleared all foreign troops out of Russia.

After the war

Famine added to Russia's miseries. In August 1921, in a desperate attempt to grow more food, Lenin abandoned one of the main principles of the Revolution. Limited private

The changes did not satisfy Lenin and his Bolsheviks and in mid-July they staged an armed uprising against the Provisional Government. It failed. Lenin was accused of being a German agent and fled to safety in neighbouring Finland.

Kerensky and Trotsky

On 25 July, a lawyer, Alexander Kerensky, became prime minister at the head of a weak and divided government. Petrograd, the capital, was the centre of opposition to him. Lenin returned there in October to find that a second revolution had already been planned by Lev Trotsky, the leading figure of the Petrograd Soviet. On 6

November (25 October in the old Russian calendar), Trotsky set the revolt in motion. Soon the city was in the hands of the workers and their allies, the soldiers and sailors of Russia's armed forces.

Lenin seizes power

After the revolt, Lenin came to the fore. He established a new government, called the Soviet of People's Commissars, with himself at its head. Trotsky and Joseph Stalin, the editor of *Pravda*, the party newspaper, were among its other leading figures. One of Lenin's first acts was to take Russia out of the war. Peace was signed with Germany on 3 March 1918.

Lenin was a highly effective orator. Here he addresses an audience of workers, soldiers and sailors at the Bolshevik headquarters, which had formerly been a convent school for the daughters of the nobility.

Helped to a degree by the World War I allies – Britain, France, Japan and the United States – the enemies of Communism, known as the White armies, waged war on the Red Army. Fighting was savage. Among the most disciplined troops were the sailors.

ceeded him as leader. Trotsky was first imprisoned, then exiled. In 1940 he was assassinated on Stalin's orders.

Once in power, Stalin set out to complete the Communist Revolution. Peasant landowners were forced to merge their properties into huge state-controlled farms. Millions protested and were sent to prison camps in Siberia or shot. Stalin realized that Russia would remain a second-rate power until her industries rivalled those of America and Western Europe. He pushed through a programme of rapid industrialization on a vast scale.

enterprise was permitted and peasants were once more allowed to own land.

Stalin, dictator of Russia

Meanwhile, Stalin had taken a grip on the Communist Party by placing his own people in all key positions. Thus, when Lenin died on 21 January 1924, it was Stalin, not Trotsky, who suc-

Stalin's terror

Personal freedom disappeared under Stalin. Dissenters were eliminated. Many were tortured

into 'confessions'. In the mid-thirties, Stalin disposed of his remaining rivals in sham trials or by secret execution.

In 1917, the Russian people had rebelled against the unjust government of the tsar. Twenty years later, they were governed by a regime more cruel and tyrannical than the one they had overthrown.

Trotsky was in charge of the Red Army. During the two and a half years of the Civil War his campaign headquarters – and his home – were aboard an armoured train on which he travelled.

Stalin defeated Trotsky in the struggle for leadership of the Communist Party. Stalin was ruthless, destroying personal freedoms and enforcing peasant labour more brutally than any previous regime.

World War II

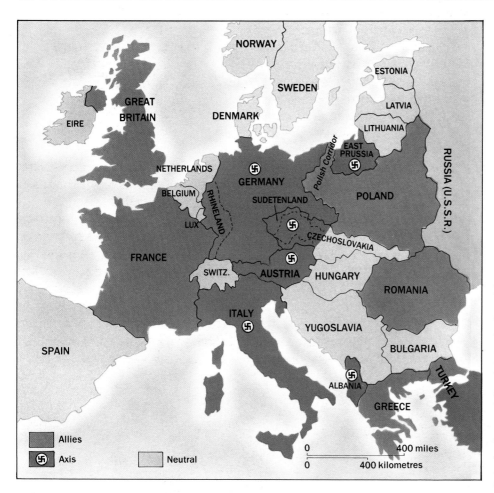

In spring 1941, Denmark fell in a single day. By the end of May, Holland and Belgium had been overrun and Norway had been occupied. On 21 June, France surrendered. Most of the British army in France escaped to Britain from the beaches of Dunkirk.

The Battle of Britain
The conquest of Britain was Hitler's next objective. Command of the air over the Channel was essential to his plan, to allow German troops to be landed in Britain in safety.

First, he ordered the German air force – the Luftwaffe – to destroy Britain's Royal Air Force. The battle began in early August 1940 and continued without pause into September. The Luftwaffe's losses mounted, yet the RAF seemed as strong as ever. In mid-September Hitler called off the invasion and switched his tactics to

The coming of war
In 1933, the Nazi leader, Adolf Hitler, became Chancellor of Germany. Hitler aimed to make Germany supreme in Europe. In 1938 he occupied part of Czechoslovakia and seized the whole of Austria.

In August 1939, Germany invaded Poland. Britain and France were Poland's allies. They demanded that Hitler should withdraw his troops, but he ignored them. On 3 September 1939, Britain and France declared war on Germany, but they were unable to save the Poles. Poland was overwhelmed in 18 days.

Blitzkrieg and the fall of France
A new kind of war, blitzkrieg – 'lightning war' – was the key to Germany's success. Fast-moving tanks and motorized infantry backed by aircraft in great numbers smashed all opposition.

Map: Europe at the outbreak of World War II. When no one tried to stop him, Hitler believed it was safe to grab more territory. He attacked Poland in 1939 in the hope of joining together the two parts of Germany, which had been separated since World War I.

Germany and her European allies were known as the Axis.

Adolf Hitler was the leader of Germany. He kept himself in power by terrorizing everyone who opposed him. Millions of Jews were killed under his orders.

bombing Britain by night. The raids caused much damage and thousands of civilian casualties, but Britain had been saved from invasion. It was a turning point in the war.

The invasion of the USSR

Foiled in his attempt to conquer Britain, Hitler planned to invade the USSR. Three million Germans were massed on the Russian border. On 22 June, the invasion began.

The Soviet army was soon in retreat. Half the Soviet air force was destroyed and, by 30 September, the Germans were near Moscow, the Soviet capital. Bad weather saved the Russians. Rain turned Russia's dirt roads into rivers of mud and the German tanks were halted. Then winter came. The Germans were totally unprepared for it. Men froze to death and the icy conditions made tanks and guns unusable.

The Russians were equipped to fight in winter. Their armies were reinforced by millions of recruits from the USSR's Asian territories. On 6 December, Marshal Zhukov, the Soviet Army commander, counter-attacked. The Germans retreated. Moscow was saved.

Winston Churchill's speeches inspired the British and defied the Nazis: 'We shall fight on the beaches, we shall fight on the landing-grounds, we shall fight in the fields and in the streets, we shall fight in the hills. We shall NEVER surrender.'

The German army marches triumphantly through the Arc de Triomphe in Paris in 1940. General Charles de Gaulle (centre) led the Free French resistance from London. His broadcasts gave the French courage and hope of liberation from German occupation.

Marshal Georgi Zhukov was the mastermind behind the Russian defeat of the German armies which attacked on three fronts using blitzkrieg warfare. He was known as the 'general who never lost a battle'.

Enter Japan and the USA

During the 1930s Japan had conquered Korea, Manchuria and huge areas of China. In 1940, after the fall of France, she occupied French colonies in Southeast Asia.

Japan's expansion threatened American and British interests in the area. Talks to settle the disagreements that had arisen were still in progress when, on 7 December 1941, Japanese aircraft launched a surprise attack on the US Pacific fleet anchored in Pearl Harbor, Hawaii. The United States and Britain and her allies immediately declared war on Japan.

With the US fleet temporarily disabled, the Japanese could do as they liked. Swiftly they seized the Philippines, Malaya, Singapore, Hong Kong, Burma,

the Dutch East Indies and numerous Pacific islands.

The Battle of the Atlantic

Vital supplies for Britain were shipped across the Atlantic. German submarines – U-boats – came close to cutting this supply life-line. But in time, using improved weapons and with American help, the British managed to beat the U-boat threat.

War in the desert

Italy had entered the war on Germany's side on 10 June 1940. In September, an Italian army invaded Egypt. The small British force guarding the Suez Canal drove the Italians off. It was the beginning of the war in the North African desert.

In early 1941, German troops commanded by General Erwin Rommel arrived in North Africa. For the next year, the battle moved to and fro across the desert. By October 1942, the Germans had advanced into Egypt. They threatened the Suez Canal, but were defeated at El Alamein and driven back into Libya by Britain's Eighth Army under a new commander, General Montgomery.

On 8 November 1942, American and British troops com-

A German town lies in ruins. By late 1944, RAF Bomber Command was capable of terrifying destruction. In a single raid on Darmstadt, 218 Lancaster bombers killed over 8000 people and utterly devastated half the town.

President Franklin Delano Roosevelt led the United States to victory in war and made his country the most powerful nation in history. When first elected he declared: 'The only thing we have to fear is fear itself.'

Defeat in Russia

In spring 1942, when better weather returned to Russia, Hitler ordered his armies to capture Stalingrad, the great industrial city on the River Volga. Hitler directed the campaign himself, from headquarters in Germany.

manded by the American general Eisenhower, landed in North Africa. They moved east into Tunisia to attack the Germans retreating after El Alamein in the rear. Fresh German troops flown in from Italy merely delayed the inevitable end. On 12 May 1943, German and Italian forces in North Africa surrendered. The desert war was over.

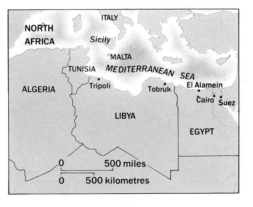

NORTH AFRICA
ITALY
Sicily
MALTA
TUNISIA
MEDITERRANEAN SEA
ALGERIA
Tripoli
Tobruk
El Alamein
Cairo Suez
LIBYA
EGYPT

0   500 miles
0   500 kilometres

Stalingrad became a German graveyard. A gigantic Russian pincer movement encircled the city. In February 1943, the surviving German troops gave themselves up.

Throughout 1943, the Russians advanced on all fronts. In January 1944, they freed Leningrad from a siege that had lasted 890 days. The Russian

The US Fleet on fire at Pearl Harbor. The Japanese surprised the Allies with their skill in warfare and the quality of their weapons. With ten fast, modern aircraft carriers and 2600 warplanes, they were able to win all the early battles of the Pacific War.

Map: The Desert War was begun by Italian dictator Mussolini who wanted control of the Suez Canal. Fighting moved back and forth along the North African coast for two years. From bases in North Africa, the Allies invaded Italy in 1943 and liberated Rome in 1944.

General Montgomery (left) defeated the Germans and Italians, led by Field Marshal Rommel (right), at El Alamein in 1942. Under General Eisenhower the Allies forced the Italians and the German Afrika Korps to surrender completely in 1943.

armies rolled on through the countries of Eastern Europe, which had been seized by Hitler. In all of them, the Russians set up Communist regimes. Thus, even before the war was over, Europe was being divided between East and West.

The end of Hitler's Europe

From 1943, Germany was bombed round the clock by American and British aircraft. The severe and widespread destruction caused failed to break German morale or to inflict mortal damage on Germany's war effort. The war had to be won on the ground and the Allies prepared to invade the continent of Europe.

Early on 6 June 1944, Allied forces landed on the beaches of Normandy. After fierce fighting they established a bridgehead on the French coast and began the advance through France towards Germany. By mid-December 1944, American troops had reached the Rhine. They were preparing to cross

the river into Germany when an unexpected counter-attack drove them back into France. It was a temporary setback. The Allies resumed their advance and from then on nothing could save Germany from defeat.

In spring 1945, the Allies closed in on Germany from the west, while the Russians advanced in the east. On 30

General Dwight D. Eisenhower, Supreme Commander of Allied Forces, commanded Operation Overlord, the invasion of Europe. Altogether three million troops were involved, plus 10,000 aircraft, 1200 warships and over 5000 transports and landing craft.

Early on 6 June 1944, warships and bombers battered the massive German defences in Normandy, France. At 6.30am the first assault troops went ashore. Landing craft went right up the beaches to deliver food, ammunition, tanks, lorries and self-propelled guns.

General George Patton led the American advance across France. His toughness and plain-speaking earned him the nickname 'old blood and guts'.

April, Hitler killed himself in his underground bunker in Berlin. On 8 May, Germany surrendered.

The collapse of Japan

By lucky chance, the aircraft carriers in the US Pacific fleet had been at sea when the Japanese bombed Pearl Harbor and so escaped destruction. Those carriers and others which joined them won the naval war in the Pacific.

In June 1942, at the Battle of Midway, the Americans sank all four aircraft carriers in the opposing Japanese fleet. After that decisive victory, the long, hard task began of recapturing the territories seized by the Japanese during the first six months of 1942.

Indian and British troops prevented the Japanese from invading India. Australia was saved from invasion by a combined Australian and American force which cleared the Japanese out of New Guinea.

The atomic bomb

As the Americans tightened the noose around Japan, every one of the islands they captured was defended by soldiers who chose to die rather than surrender. US military planners estimated that at least a million American troops would be killed in the invasion of Japan itself. The alternative to invasion was to use the newly developed atomic bomb. The Americans reckoned

that the fearsome destruction it was likely to cause would compel the Japanese to ask for peace.

Hiroshima was attacked on 6 August 1945. A single atomic bomb wiped out most of the city. Then, on 9 August, a second bomb devastated Nagasaki. On 14 August, Japan surrendered. World War II was over.

After the war

Britain and France were gravely weakened by the war. Their huge empires split up into a host of independent nations. The United States and the USSR emerged from the war as superpowers. But their wartime friendship turned to enmity and divided the whole world into two hostile groups.

On 6 August 1945, the Allies dropped the first atom bomb on Japan. It destroyed Hiroshima and killed more than 70,000 people. A second bomb dropped on Nagasaki killed about 40,000. Many more died of burns, wounds and radiation sickness.

Wars of Modern Times

The Spanish Civil War

Opposing sides At first, Spanish army generals v Spanish government. Later, Fascists v Socialists (both from many countries).

Cause Spanish generals oppose left-wing policies of Republican Government. They set out to overthrow it.

Major figure General Franco.

Battleground Spain.

Main events 1936 July: Army rebellion. September: Italy and Germany support rebels. Russia aids Government. October: Franco appointed rebel leader. November: Rebels besiege the capital, Madrid. 1937 February: They capture Malaga. March: Italians routed at Guadalajara. April: Germans bomb Guernica – an undefended city. World opinion shocked. Government planes sink rebel battleship. June: Rebels capture Bilbao. August-July: Government attacks near Madrid and in Aragon fail. 1938 February-June: Rebels advance east to the sea and split Government-held territory in two. July: Government tries to recapture lost territory but fails. 1939

January: Rebels capture Barcelona. March: They take Madrid. War ends. Rebels victorious.

Outcome Franco rules as dictator. His success convinces Hitler and Mussolini that aggression pays. It is a step on the road to World War II.

The Korean War

Opposing sides North Korea supported by Russia and China v South Korea supported by United Nations (principally the USA).

Causes Rivalry between North Koreans and South Koreans to dominate the whole country.

Major figures Generals MacArthur and Ridgway. President Truman.

Battleground Korea.

Main events 1950 June: North Korean Army (NKA) invades and overruns the South. (United Nations recommends members to support the South. Fifteen nations send troops. They fight under US command.) UN force limited to small area around Pusan. September: UN lands force at Inchon and breaks out of Pusan.

NKA in full retreat. October: UN force reaches Chinese border, on River Yalu. Huge numbers of Chinese troops sent to aid NKA. They drive UN force south of 38th parallel. 1951 January-February UN counter-attack slowly regains lost ground. June: UN command establishes line of defences north of 38th parallel. War settles into stalemate. July: Peace talks begin and drag on for two years. 1953 July: Armistice signed.

Outcome Korea divided along line where fighting stopped. UN's casualties 383,000. Opponents lose 1,600,000 men.

The Cuban Missile Crisis

Opposing sides USA v USSR.

Major figures US president John F. Kennedy v USSR prime minister Khrushchev.

Scene of crisis Cuba.

Main events 1962 September: USSR admits supplying arms to Cuba but maintains they are for defence only. 16 October: US aircraft over Cuba take photos showing missiles with nuclear warheads ready for firing. Missiles capable of hitting US cities. More known to be on the way in Russian ships. 22 October: Kennedy announces US fleet will blockade Cuba to prevent more missiles arriving. 23 October: At United Nations, US demands that Russians dismantle Cuban missile bases. Oct 23: US and USSR forces on full alert. 26 October: Khrushchev offers to withdraw Cuban missiles if US and NATO allies remove nuclear missiles from Turkey. US refuses. Nuclear war seems likely. 28 October: Khrushchev agrees to withdraw missiles if US lifts naval blockade and undertakes not to invade Cuba. 2 November: US lifts blockade as USSR removes missiles. Crisis ends.

Outcome US and USSR realize that crisis almost led to nuclear war. 'Hot line' installed between Washington and Moscow to allow quick and direct communication between leaders.

Hundreds of thousands of Spanish civilians died during the Spanish Civil War. Volunteers, including women, flocked to join the Socialist cause, but the Fascists, supported by Hitler and Mussolini, triumphed and installed General Franco as dictator of Spain.

The Nigerian Civil War

Opposing sides Ibo people of Nigeria (Biafra) v the rest of Nigeria.
Causes Ibos determine to break away from Nigeria and set up an independent state they call 'Biafra'.
Leaders Ibos: Colonel Ojukwu. Federation of Nigeria: General Gowon.
Battleground Eastern Nigeria.
Main events 1967 May: Ojukwu announces formation of Biafra. June: Gowon reorganizes Nigeria as a Federation and invites Biafra to join. Ojukwu refuses. 7 June: Federal troops invade Biafra. 13 July: They take university town of Nsukka. Biafrans counter-attack. A mobile force gets to within 160 km (100 miles) of Federal capital Lagos. Lack of support forces it to turn back. September: Federal troops continue to push forward into Biafra. 4 October: They capture Enugu, capital of Biafra. 1968 May: Biafrans cut off from the sea and surrounded by Federal forces. They fight on. Foreign sympathizers send supplies by air. 1970 January: Federal army captures Owerri, last Biafran stronghold. Ojukwu flees. 12 January: Ceasefire agreed. War ends.
Outcome Nigeria remains united.

The Falklands War

Opposing sides Britain v Argentina.
Causes Argentina claims the Falklands. Britain rejects claim. Argentina decides to take Falklands by force.
Battleground Falkland Islands.
Main events 1982 2 April: 2,000 Argentine troops invade the Falklands. They overcome the 18-strong British garrison. Argentina also captures South Georgia. 3 April: United Nations calls on Argentines to withdraw. They refuse and land 18,000 more troops. 5 April: British task force sails to recapture the islands. 25 April: British reoccupy South Georgia. 1 May: First British air attacks on Argentine positions on Falklands. 2 May: British submarine sinks Argentine cruiser *Belgrano*. 368 Argentines killed. May 4: Argentine planes disable British cruiser *Sheffield*. 21 May: British land at San Carlos. Argentines sink British frigates. 31 May: British now firmly established on Falklands. June: They advance on capital Port Stanley. 14 June: Port Stanley captured. Argentines surrender. 225 British and 725 Argentines die in war.
Outcome Falklands remain British.

The Gulf War

Opposing sides Iraq v United Nations (principally USA, Saudi Arabia, Britain, France).
Causes Iraqi seizure of Kuwait.
Iraqi leader Saddam Hussein.
Battlegrounds Kuwait, Iraq.
Main events 1990 2 August: Iraqis occupy Kuwait. 6 August: UN tells all members to cease trade with Iraq. 29 November: UN orders Iraq to withdraw from Kuwait by 15 January 1991 or be forced out. November-December: US and 28 other UN members build up Kuwait liberation force. 1991 16 January: Iraq still occupies Kuwait. UN air forces make daily raids on targets throughout Iraq. 17 January: Iraqis commence long-range missile strikes on Israel. 24 January: Ecological disaster threatened by massive oil flows from oil wells and terminals blown up by Iraqis. 27 January: 142 Iraqi warplanes flee to Iran. 24 February: UN ground offensive begins. Iraqis show little fight. 26 February: UN force frees Kuwait City. Iraqis in full retreat. 28 February: Ceasefire ends fighting.
Outcome Kuwait liberated. Iraq rejects parts of peace settlement and UN applies sanctions. Saddam Hussein crushes internal revolts and remains in power.

British paratroopers defend a beach in the Falkland Islands during the 1982 conflict. The Argentines claim the Islas Malvinas as their own, though the tiny population of the islands would rather they remained British.

Saddam Hussein's threat to set the desert alight in a blaze that would burn for years was not realized. His defeated troops did fire the oil wells, and massive economic and environmental damage was caused, but US firefighters managed to cap all the wells and put out the fires.

The Vietnam War

Defeat of the French

France had ruled Indochina since the 1800s. During World War II, Japan occupied Vietnam and the other French colonies in Indochina. After Japan's defeat

in 1945, the French returned to Vietnam. They found that an independent government had already been set up in the north by Ho Chi Minh, a lifelong Communist and pre-war leader of the movement for Vietnamese independence.

The French recognized Ho's regime in North Vietnam but established a separate government in the South. Years of war between Communist North Vietnam and the French-supported South followed. The French abandoned Vietnam after suffering a crushing defeat by the Communists, at Dien Bien Phu, in May 1954.

Vietnam divided

Vietnam then became two independent states, North and South Vietnam. The North, under Ho Chi Minh, was committed to uniting the whole of Vietnam into a single Communist state. The world's anti-Communist powers, led by the United States, wished to keep the South independent. They feared that if South Vietnam became Communist the rest of Southeast Asia would become Communist too.

The South Vietnamese government was both corrupt and unpopular. An underground Communist movement, the Viet Cong, with support from the North, won control of huge areas of the country apart from

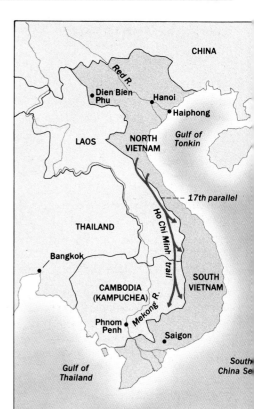

During the Vietnam War the South Vietnamese Communists were inspired and encouraged by Ho Chi Minh, the president of Communist North Vietnam. When the city of Saigon eventually fell, it was renamed Ho Chi Minh City.

In 1965 President Johnson sent US Marines into Vietnam. Landed by sea, they were the first American land troops. By 1969 there were 540,000 US troops in Vietnam.

Map: The Vietnam War was fought mainly in North and South Vietnam, but it spread to neighbouring Laos, Cambodia (Kampuchea) and Thailand. The Ho Chi Minh trail ran the length of South Vietnam but was safely over the border.

the towns. By 1964, South Vietnam seemed about to fall into Communist hands.

The USA enters the war

In 1964, the United States became really entangled in the struggle in Vietnam. In August that year, North Vietnamese torpedo boats attacked American destroyers in the Gulf of Tonkin. American aircraft retaliated by bombing military targets in the North.

America's President Lyndon B. Johnson announced a programme of military aid for South Vietnam and sent numbers of American military advisers to serve with the South Vietnamese forces. Early in 1965, the Viet Cong killed several of these advisers in an attack on a barracks near Saigon. The US replied by bombing North Vietnam.

By June 1966, as many as 265,000 Americans were serving in Vietnam with thousands more on the way. An American fleet patrolled the coast, preventing supplies for the North coming by sea.

The US commanders believed that they could bomb the North into defeat. A bombing campaign code-named 'Rolling Thunder' began in March 1965. It caused immense destruction and horrendous casualties, but the Communists fought on. After three years the Americans had to admit that bombing had failed. On 31 March 1968, 'Rolling Thunder' was called off.

Guerrilla war

The war on the ground was also going badly for the United States. The country as a whole was ruled by the Viet Cong guerrillas. The American troops in South Vietnam commanded little more than the bases they lived in. The Viet Cong tactics were to hide, hit and run and the Americans found it very difficult to catch them.

North Vietnam supplied the Viet Cong via the Ho Chi Minh trail. The trail followed the Vietnamese border, but not on the Vietnamese side. It lay in neutral territory, so the Americans shrank from attacking it

Operation Rolling Thunder was a failed attempt to force the North Vietnamese to withdraw from South Vietnam. Using mostly B52 bombers (shown here), the United States rained nearly 900,000 tonnes of bombs on to North Vietnam.

by land. They tried instead to destroy it from the air. They pounded the trail with bombs and killed the foliage that hid it with chemical sprays, but in vain. The trail remained open.

The Tet Offensive
However, the military might of the United States slowly wore down Communist resistance. Americans at home were told

that the war was being won. But the Viet Cong were not finished. In January 1968, during Vietnam's Tet festival, they launched over 100 attacks on American targets.

Within a week the Americans and South Vietnamese had recovered their losses. But the

American public had had enough. The movement to take America out of the war became irresistible.

America gets out of the war
In June 1969, Richard Nixon, the new American President, announced that American forces were going to leave Vietnam. But in 1970, North Vietnam invaded its neighbour, Cambodia. American troops crossed the border to aid the Cambodians, but this widening of the war aroused so much protest in America that they were promptly withdrawn.

With fewer American troops to contend with, the North Vietnamese regular army invaded the South. The US responded with bombing that threatened to destroy the entire

economy of the North. The Communists asked for a truce and on 30 December 1972, the American bombing ceased. On 27 January 1973, the United States signed an agreement to end the conflict. In March, the last American troops left for home.

American aid for the South dwindled while the North received increasing help from the Soviet Union. In January 1975, North Vietnamese troops launched a full-scale invasion of the South. On 30 April, they captured the capital, Saigon. The Communist victory was complete.

Continuing conflict
In 1975, supported by Communist China, the Communist Khmer Rouge had seized power in Cambodia. Repeated border clashes with the Khmer Rouge led, in 1978, to the Vietnamese invading Cambodia, where they defeated the Khmer Rouge and set up a new government. The Khmer Rouge went under-

General Giap (top) was the Communists' military genius. He learned the skills of guerrilla warfare from the Chinese communist leader Mao Tse-Tung.

Three presidents: John F. Kennedy (left) ordered the first big build-up of military power in Vietnam. Lyndon B. Johnson (centre) was so unpopular after the Tet Offensive that he did not seek re-election in 1968. Richard M. Nixon finally pulled US troops out.

Thousands of tonnes of supplies were bicycled down the Ho Chi Minh trail. Besides jungles, mountains and rivers, the guerrillas had to cope with napalm and other chemical weapons that the Americans used to strip the cover from their tracks and hiding places.

ground and continued the war against the Vietnamese.

In 1979, the Chinese invaded Vietnam as a reprisal for the overthrow of the Khmer Rouge. They did as much damage as they could and then withdrew.

The fruits of war

The United States was shamed by its failure in Vietnam. The war deeply divided the American people and ruined the lives of many Americans who fought in it.

Thousands of people in former South Vietnam lost their lives as they fled abroad by sea to escape the Communist regime. The Vietnamese faced years of poverty as they strove to rebuild their country devastated by decades of war.

A Communist soldier waves the North Vietnamese flag in triumph over a captured US bunker. On 30 April 1975 the North Vietnamese captured Saigon. The last guards at the American Embassy were airlifted off the roof as looters broke down the main door.

The Arab-Israeli Wars

The roots of conflict

In 1918, when World War I ended, Palestine had been part of the Ottoman empire for 400 years. The land was inhabited mainly by Arabs with a small number of Jews. During the war the British had promised to support the foundation of a Jewish homeland in Palestine. They also led the Arabs to believe that Palestine would remain in Arab hands.

The Ottoman empire was split up after the war and the League of Nations granted Britain the mandate to govern Palestine. More Jews settled and in 1936 Arab anger at the growth in the Jewish population boiled over into revolt.

After World War II, thousands of homeless Jews sought refuge in Palestine. Jewish terrorists attacked both British and Arab targets when Britain, bowing to Arab pressure, restricted the numbers of Jewish immigrants. In 1947, Britain announced that she was handing over responsibility for Palestine to the United Nations. On 14 May 1948, as the last British troops left, the Jewish leader David Ben-Gurion proclaimed the new state of Israel.

The Palestine War (1948)

Within hours of the British departure, Arab armies from Egypt, Transjordan (now Jordan), Iraq, Syria and Lebanon invaded Israel. In the chaotic fighting that followed, a cease-fire arranged by the UN saved the Israelis, who were on the point of running out of money and supplies. The Israelis used the lull in the conflict to collect funds to continue the war from Jews around the world. The generous response, particularly from America, rescued Israel from collapse.

Fighting resumed in October and gradually the Israelis gained the upper hand. The war ended in early 1949. It left the

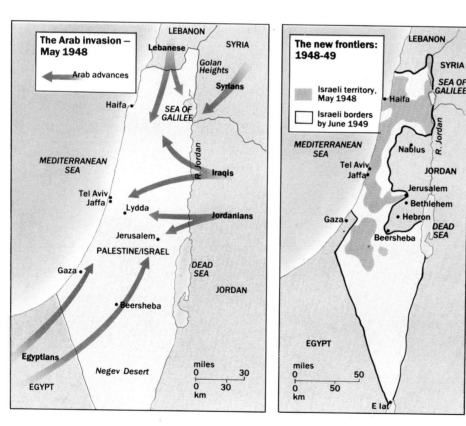

Maps: In 1948, after the British and United Nations departed, Israel was invaded by armies from Egypt, Transjordan (now Jordan), Iraq, Syria and Lebanon (left). By the end of the war (right), Israel had gained three-quarters of Palestine. Only the Gaza strip, the West Bank and part of Jerusalem remained in Arab hands. But Israel was hardly secure. Near Tel Aviv the country was only 15 kilometres wide.

On 14 May 1948, in Tel Aviv, David Ben-Gurion, the Prime Minister, declared Israel independent. That same evening the Arabs invaded. The flag of Israel shows the Star of David and its colours are those of the traditional shawl which Jews wear at prayer.

Israelis masters of three-quarters of Palestine.

To both Israelis and Arabs, the ceasefire was merely a pause in the fighting. Thousands of Arabs had fled to nearby Arab states to escape the Israeli occupation. Their settlements lining the frontiers with Israel soon degenerated into squalid shanty towns. The refugees who inhabited them waged perpetual guerrilla war against the new Israeli state.

The Suez War (1956)

While the Israelis received aid from America, Egypt's leader Gamal Abdul Nasser rebuilt his armed forces with Soviet help. On 26 July 1956, he seized con-

trol of the Suez Canal from Britain and France. In an effort to recover the canal from the Egyptians, Britain and France sought Israeli cooperation. On 29 October 1956, Israeli troops invaded Egypt and advanced towards the canal. On 5 November, French and British forces landed at the mouth of the

canal on the pretext that they had come to protect it. Violently hostile reaction from the rest of the world forced them and the Israelis to withdraw. The attack on Egypt collapsed.

The United Nations estimated that 656,000 Arabs fled from Palestine to neighbouring Arab states. They became people without a country, forced to live in poverty and squalor. The refugee settlements became bases from which Arab guerrillas struck at Israel.

Gamal Abdul Nasser seized the Suez Canal in 1956. Israel, Britain and France conspired to attack the Egyptians. They took many prisoners and captured huge quantities of arms and ammunition. But world opinion was outraged and they withdrew.

Arabs demonstrate their opposition to Israel. In 1964 the Palestine Liberation Organization was set up to unite all Palestinian refugees. The guerrilla movement Al Fatah continually harassed the Israelis.

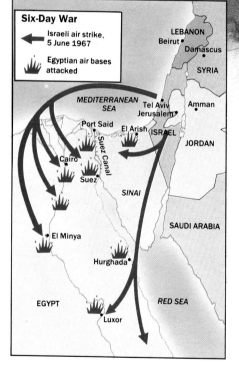

Six-Day War

← Israeli air strike, 5 June 1967

🔥 Egyptian air bases attacked

LEBANON
Beirut ·
· Damascus
SYRIA
MEDITERRANEAN SEA
Tel Aviv ·
Jerusalem ·
· Amman
Port Said ·
El Arish · ISRAEL
JORDAN
Cairo ·
Suez ·
SINAI
El Minya ·
SAUDI ARABIA
Hurghada ·
EGYPT
RED SEA
Luxor ·

Israel after the Six-Day War

■ Israel, 1949-67

▨ Israeli occupied 1967

LEBANON
SYRIA
GOLAN HEIGHTS
MEDITERRANEAN SEA
WEST BANK
· Jericho
Jerusalem ·
GAZA STRIP
ISRAEL
JORDAN
Suez Canal
SINAI
Israeli control of small oil fields
Eilat ·
SAUDI ARABIA
EGYPT
Sharm-el-Sheikh ·

The Six-Day War (1967)

Several years of unrest in the Arab world followed. Egypt remained the strongest Arab state and in 1967, goaded by his fellow Arabs, Nasser called for a Muslim holy war against Israel. The Israelis struck first. In separate actions between 5 and 10 June, they virtually eliminated the armed forces of Egypt, Jordan and Syria.

Israel's size trebled as a result of her victories. Thousands more Palestinians fled abroad but nearly a million remained in the conquered territories where they became a source of endless trouble to the Israelis. In 1964, the Palestine Liberation Organization, (the PLO) had been founded to co-ordinate the Arab struggle against Israel. In 1969, Yasser Arafat, leader of the much-feared Al Fatah guerrilla group, became its head.

The Six-Day War: Every morning, Egyptian aircraft flew dawn patrols and then returned to refuel. Knowing this, the Israelis timed their strike force to arrive just after these aircraft had landed. They destroyed over 400 planes on the ground.

Maps: The Israeli aircraft confused the Egyptian defences (left) by making a wide sweep out over the sea before homing in for the attack. The land Israel won in the war (right) made her frontiers more secure.

The Yom Kippur War (1973)

With Soviet help, Egypt, led by Nasser's successor Anwar Sadat, re-armed once again. On 6 October 1973, as all Israel celebrated the festival of Yom Kippur, Egyptian and Syrian armies attacked Israeli border positions. The Israelis at first gave ground, but counter-attacked and drove the invaders back. The two superpowers, America and the Soviet Union, now took a hand. They put pressure on the warring sides to end a conflict which, it was feared, might set off a third world war. A ceasefire was agreed on 24 October.

After a period of complex diplomacy led by America's Secretary of State Henry Kissinger, Israelis and Egyptians finally came together at a meeting chaired by America's President Jimmy Carter. In March 1979, at Camp David, they signed a formal peace treaty.

War with Lebanon

Border warfare between Israelis and Palestinian groups, now based in Lebanon, went on. In 1982, to put an end to repeated cross-border attacks, the Israelis

invaded Lebanon. They besieged the Lebanese capital Beirut and its Syrian garrison. It took armed American intervention to head off a full-scale war between Syria and Israel. In 1985, the Israelis withdrew to their own frontiers.

The Intifada

Early in 1988, Palestinians living in Israeli-occupied territory rose in revolt. The Arabs called it 'Intifada' – the uprising. Riots, bombings and other acts of violence against the Israelis have continued ever since.

Hopes for peace

In September 1993, after months of secret talks in Norway, the PLO leaders and Israel at last accepted the other's right to exist. Israel handed over Gaza and the city of Jericho to the PLO as the nucleus of a Palestinian state. Both parties agreed to work for a far-reaching and permanent settlement. However, a final end to the conflict is by no means certain. Most Palestinians and Israelis welcome the promise of peace, but extremists on both sides have condemned the agreement and continue the struggle.

Moshe Dayan, who lost an eye while fighting for the British in Syria in World War II, was Israel's military genius. He fought in the Palestine War, led Israeli forces in the Suez War and, as Minister of Defence, planned Israel's successful Six-Day War campaign.

An Israeli soldier prays. It is the Day of Atonement, Yom Kippur, the holiest day of the Jewish calendar. The Egyptians deliberately chose this day for a combined Egyptian-Syrian attack on Israel. The war helped bring about the Camp David peace talks.

Yasser Arafat formed the Al Fatah guerrilla group in 1956. In 1969 he became president of the PLO. Seen as a terrorist by some, a statesman by others, he signed an agreement recognizing Israel's right to exist in 1993.

The Future of Warfare

The revolution in science and technology has changed the practice of warfare beyond recognition during the past hundred years. Technological competition on land, sea, air and now in space has intensified without interruption. New materials, huge improvements in communications, new advanced weapons and weapon systems offer possibilities hitherto not dreamed of. Today's rate of change is so rapid that neither political nor military leaders can absorb fully the significance of what is happening. There is little evidence on which to base attempts to foresee the action that will take place on the battlefields of the future.

Cold war ends, civil wars start

Recent changes in the political balance of the world have been as revolutionary and as fundamental as those in technology. In November 1989, the German people breached the Berlin Wall that divided their country and in so doing signalled the collapse of old-style Communism. The demolition of this symbol

The United Nations flag has a map of the world surrounded by a wreath of olive branches to symbolize peace.

With the ending of the cold war, the threat of global nuclear war has diminished, but in its place has come the certainty of bitter local conflicts. The casualties of these civil wars are mostly innocent civilians caught up in the fighting.

of world division foreshadowed the disintegration of the Soviet Union and finally ended the threat of a nuclear world war between the Communist East and the Democratic West.

The optimism that a general peace might follow these stirring events was short-lived. Bitter and bloody local conflicts have replaced global hostility. The United Nations was praised for its role in upholding international justice and order in the Gulf War in the Middle East but its powers as a peace-keeper and peace-maker in what are effectively civil wars is in doubt.

The continuing strife in parts of Africa, Asia, the Caribbean and in the former Yugoslavia has demonstrated the inability of the UN to impose peace on people whose leaders and armies are determined to go on fighting. It also appears likely that the wealthier nations of the world, those on whom the UN has always depended to carry out its policies, will provide support for the UN only when and where their particular interests are in peril.

Zones of peace and war

For almost half a century, suspicion and fear split the international community into two hostile camps. It has been suggested that the world is now drifting towards a new kind of division. On the one hand there will be 'zones of peace' and on the other, 'zones of turmoil'. The rich countries will remain reasonably pleasant places, relatively tranquil and free of major violence. The rest, representing over 60 per cent of the globe, will exist in a state of more or less continuous war and unrest. The fortunate 40 per cent will know what is going on in the less fortunate parts of the world. They will care but they will simply be unable to stop it.

The United Nations' ability to maintain peace is limited. Peacekeeping forces are sent in only when both sides in a conflict agree to them, and many countries are loath to risk the lives of their own troops in a conflict that does not directly concern them.

Index

Numerals in *italics* refer to picture captions.